AF350472

Mastering Pygame: From Basics to Advanced Game Development

Kameron Hussain and Frahaan Hussain

Published by Kameron Hussain, 2024.

While every precaution has been taken in the preparation of this book, the publisher assumes no responsibility for errors or omissions, or for damages resulting from the use of the information contained herein.

MASTERING PYGAME: FROM BASICS TO ADVANCED GAME DEVELOPMENT

First edition. April 16, 2024.

Copyright © 2024 Kameron Hussain and Frahaan Hussain.

ISBN: 979-8223060185

Written by Kameron Hussain and Frahaan Hussain.

Table of Contents

Phaser

Other Frameworks and Engines

Transitioning from Pygame to More Advanced Engines

Further Learning Resources

Building a Portfolio and Getting Involved in the Industry

Future Trends in Game Development

Chapter 1: Introduction to Pygame

1.1 Overview of Pygame and Its Capabilities

Pygame is a popular Python library used for creating games. It builds upon the SDL (Simple DirectMedia Layer) library, providing a simple interface to access various multimedia functionalities. With Pygame, developers can easily create games with 2D graphics, handle input events, play sounds, and more.

At its core, Pygame offers a set of modules that abstract low-level tasks, allowing developers to focus on game logic rather than implementation details. Some of the key capabilities of Pygame include:

- **Graphics:** Pygame provides functions for drawing shapes, images, and text on the screen. Developers can create visually appealing games using these graphics primitives.

- **Input Handling:** Pygame simplifies the process of handling user input from keyboards, mice, and joysticks. This makes it easy to implement player controls and interaction in games.

- **Audio:** Sound effects and background music are essential for immersive gaming experiences. Pygame offers functionalities for loading and playing audio files, enabling developers to add audio elements to their games.

- **Window Management:** Pygame abstracts window creation and management, making it straightforward to create resizable windows, handle fullscreen mode, and manage display settings.

- **Event Handling:** Events such as key presses, mouse movements, and window events are fundamental for game interactivity. Pygame provides mechanisms to detect and respond to these events, allowing developers to create responsive games.

Pygame's simplicity and ease of use make it an excellent choice for beginners learning game development in Python. Additionally, its versatility and extensibility make it suitable for creating both simple prototypes and complex, polished games.

With a vibrant community and extensive documentation, Pygame continues to evolve, with new features and improvements regularly added by contributors worldwide. Whether you're a hobbyist experimenting with game development or a professional building commercial games, Pygame provides a solid foundation for bringing your game ideas to life.

1.2 Setting Up the Pygame Environment

SETTING UP THE PYGAME environment is the first step towards creating games with Pygame. Before diving into game development, it's essential to ensure that Pygame is installed and configured correctly on your system. Here's a guide to setting up Pygame:

Installing Pygame

TO INSTALL PYGAME, you can use pip, the Python package manager. Open a terminal or command prompt and run the following command:

pip install pygame

This command will download and install Pygame and its dependencies automatically. Make sure you have an active internet connection during the installation process.

Verifying the Installation

ONCE PYGAME IS INSTALLED, you can verify the installation by running a simple script. Create a new Python file and add the following code:

import pygame

 # Initialize Pygame

pygame.init()

 # Set up the display

screen = pygame.display.set_mode((800, 600))

```python
pygame.display.set_caption("Pygame Installation Test")

# Main loop

running = True

while running:

for event in pygame.event.get():

if event.type == pygame.QUIT:

running = False

# Fill the screen with white

screen.fill((255, 255, 255))

# Update the display

pygame.display.flip()

# Quit Pygame

pygame.quit()
```

Save the file and run it using Python. If Pygame is installed correctly, a window should appear with a white background. You can close the window to exit the program.

IDE Integration

MANY POPULAR PYTHON integrated development environments (IDEs) support Pygame development out of the box. IDEs such as PyCharm, Visual Studio Code, and Thonny offer features like syntax highlighting, code completion, and debugging for Pygame projects.

Creating a Project

TO START A NEW PYGAME project, create a new directory for your project and organize your files accordingly. Typically, a Pygame project consists of Python scripts, image and sound files, and other assets required for the game.

Project Structure

A WELL-ORGANIZED PROJECT structure can make development more manageable. Consider structuring your project with directories for assets, scripts, and configuration files. This modular approach makes it easier to navigate and maintain your codebase as the project grows.

Documentation and Resources

PYGAME HAS EXTENSIVE documentation available online, including tutorials, guides, and reference materials. Familiarize yourself with the official Pygame documentation and explore community resources such as forums, blogs, and social media groups for additional support and inspiration.

Version Control

USING VERSION CONTROL software such as Git is essential for managing your Pygame projects. Version control allows you to track changes, collaborate with other developers, and revert to previous versions if necessary. Host your code on platforms like GitHub or GitLab to facilitate collaboration and showcase your work to the community.

1.3 Understanding the Pygame Loop

UNDERSTANDING THE PYGAME loop is crucial for developing games with Pygame. The Pygame loop, also known as the game loop, is a fundamental concept in game development that controls the flow of the game. It consists of repetitive iterations where the game updates its state, handles input, and renders graphics to the screen.

The Main Loop

AT THE HEART OF EVERY Pygame application is the main loop. This loop typically runs continuously until the game is exited by the player. Inside the loop, the game performs various tasks such as updating the game state, handling user input, and rendering graphics.

Event Handling

ONE ESSENTIAL ASPECT of the Pygame loop is event handling. Pygame allows developers to detect and respond to various events such as keyboard input, mouse movements, and window events. Event handling is typically done within the main loop using a loop that iterates over all pending events and processes them accordingly.

Updating the Game State

IN EACH ITERATION OF the main loop, the game state is updated based on player input, physics calculations, AI behavior, and other factors. This step is crucial for simulating the passage of time and keeping the game world consistent. The game state may include player positions, object properties, game scores, and more.

Rendering Graphics

AFTER UPDATING THE game state, the next step in the main loop is rendering graphics to the screen. Pygame provides functions for drawing shapes, images, and text on the screen. These graphics primitives are used to create the visual elements of the game, including player characters, enemies, backgrounds, and user interfaces.

Controlling Frame Rate

CONTROLLING THE FRAME rate is an important consideration in game development to ensure smooth and consistent gameplay. The frame rate determines how often the game updates and renders graphics per second. By default, Pygame tries to run the game loop as fast as possible, but developers can control the frame rate using techniques such as frame limiting or delta timing.

Delta Timing

DELTA TIMING IS A TECHNIQUE used to make the game loop independent of the frame rate. Instead of updating the game state and rendering graphics at fixed intervals, delta timing calculates the time elapsed since the last frame and adjusts the game logic accordingly. This helps maintain consistent gameplay across different hardware configurations and frame rates.

Exiting the Game

PROPERLY HANDLING GAME exit is essential to provide a smooth and intuitive user experience. Pygame allows developers to detect when the player closes the game window or triggers a quit event. When such events occur, the game should gracefully shut down, releasing resources and cleaning up any temporary files or data.

Optimizing the Loop

OPTIMIZING THE PYGAME loop is necessary to ensure optimal performance and responsiveness, especially in complex games with many objects and interactions. Techniques such as batching rendering operations, minimizing unnecessary calculations, and using efficient data structures can help improve the efficiency of the game loop.

Testing and Debugging

TESTING AND DEBUGGING the Pygame loop is an integral part of the game development process. Developers should thoroughly test their games under various conditions, including different hardware configurations, input devices, and operating systems. Additionally, debugging tools and techniques such as logging, assertions, and profilers can help identify and fix issues in the game loop.

1.4 Exploring Basic Pygame Functions

EXPLORING BASIC PYGAME functions is essential for getting started with game development. Pygame provides a wide range of functions and modules that simplify common tasks such as handling graphics, input, and audio. In this section, we'll explore some of the fundamental Pygame functions that every developer should be familiar with.

Initialization

THE FIRST STEP IN USING Pygame is initializing the Pygame library. This is typically done using the pygame.init() function, which initializes all the Pygame modules required for game development. It's important to call this function before using any other Pygame functions in your code.

Creating a Window

ONCE PYGAME IS INITIALIZED, you can create a window for your game using the pygame.display.set_mode() function. This function takes a tuple specifying the width and height of the window as arguments and returns a surface object representing the game window. You can then set the caption of the window using the pygame.display.set_caption() function.

Main Loop

AS DISCUSSED EARLIER, the main loop is the central component of every Pygame application. It controls the flow of the game by repeatedly updating the game state, handling user input, and rendering graphics to the screen. You can create a main loop using a while loop that runs until a certain condition is met, such as the player quitting the game.

Event Handling

EVENT HANDLING IS AN essential aspect of game development, allowing the game to respond to user input and other events. Pygame provides a convenient event loop for handling events such as key presses, mouse movements, and window events. You can iterate over all pending events using the pygame.event.get() function and process each event accordingly.

Drawing Shapes and Images

PYGAME OFFERS FUNCTIONS for drawing basic shapes such as rectangles, circles, and lines on the screen. These functions, such as pygame.draw.rect(), pygame.draw.circle(), and pygame.draw.line(), take arguments specifying the position, size, and color of the shape to be drawn. You can also load and display images using the pygame.image.load() and blit() functions.

Playing Sounds

ADDING SOUND EFFECTS and background music can enhance the gaming experience. Pygame provides functions for loading and playing audio files, including pygame.mixer.Sound() for loading sound effects and pygame.mixer.music.load() for loading background music. You can then use methods such as play() and stop() to control playback.

Handling Input

DETECTING AND PROCESSING user input is essential for creating interactive games. Pygame simplifies input handling with functions such as pygame.key.get_pressed() for detecting keyboard input and pygame.mouse.get_pos() for getting the current mouse position. You can use these functions to implement player controls and interactions in your game.

Time Management

PYGAME PROVIDES FUNCTIONS for managing time and timing-related operations. For example, you can use the pygame.time.get_ticks() function to get the current time in milliseconds, which is useful for implementing timed events and animations. Additionally, you can use functions such as pygame.time.delay() to introduce delays in your game logic.

Exiting the Game

PROPERLY EXITING THE game is essential to ensure a smooth user experience. Pygame allows you to detect when the player closes the game window or triggers a quit event using the QUIT event type. You can then use the pygame.quit() function to clean up resources and gracefully exit the game loop.

Error Handling

ERROR HANDLING IS AN important aspect of writing robust Pygame code. Pygame provides functions such as pygame.error() for handling errors and exceptions that may occur during game development. It's essential to anticipate potential errors and handle them appropriately to prevent crashes and unexpected behavior in your game.

1.5 Creating Your First Simple Game

CREATING YOUR FIRST simple game with Pygame is an exciting milestone in your journey as a game developer. In this section, we'll walk through the process of creating a basic game using Pygame, from setting up the game window to implementing player controls and adding simple gameplay mechanics.

Setting Up the Game Window

THE FIRST STEP IN CREATING a game is setting up the game window. Using Pygame, you can create a window of any size using the pygame.display.set_mode() function. Additionally, you can set the window caption using the pygame.display.set_caption() function to give your game a title.

Drawing the Game Scene

ONCE THE GAME WINDOW is set up, you can start drawing the game scene. Pygame provides functions for drawing basic shapes, images, and text on the screen. You can use these functions to create the visual elements of your game, such as player characters, enemies, backgrounds, and user interfaces.

Implementing Player Controls

PLAYER CONTROLS ARE essential for allowing the player to interact with the game. Pygame simplifies input handling with functions such as pygame.key.get_pressed() for detecting keyboard input. You can use these functions to implement controls for moving the player character, jumping, shooting, and other actions.

Adding Gameplay Mechanics

WITH THE GAME WINDOW set up and player controls implemented, you can start adding gameplay mechanics to your game. This could include features such as collision detection, scoring, health and lives systems, enemy AI, power-ups, and more. Start with simple mechanics and gradually add complexity as you become more comfortable with Pygame.

Handling Game Events

HANDLING GAME EVENTS such as collisions, score updates, and game over conditions is crucial for creating a dynamic and engaging gaming experience. Pygame allows you to detect and respond to various events using event handling techniques. For example, you can use collision detection to detect when the player collides with enemies or obstacles and respond accordingly.

Implementing Game Logic

IMPLEMENTING GAME LOGIC involves defining the rules and behaviors that govern the game world. This includes things like movement physics, enemy behavior, object interactions, and win/ lose conditions. You can use Python's object-oriented programming features to organize your code into classes and methods that represent game objects and behaviors.

Testing and Debugging

TESTING AND DEBUGGING your game is an essential part of the game development process. Pygame provides tools and techniques for testing and debugging your game, including print statements for logging messages, assertions for verifying conditions, and Pygame's built-in debugger for tracking down errors and bugs.

Refining and Polishing

ONCE THE BASIC GAMEPLAY mechanics are in place and the game is functional, you can focus on refining and polishing the game to improve its overall quality and polish. This could involve adding visual effects, sound effects, music, animations, UI elements, and other enhancements to make the game more immersive and enjoyable for players.

Getting Feedback

GETTING FEEDBACK FROM playtesters and fellow developers is invaluable for improving your game. Share your game with friends, family, and online communities, and encourage them to provide feedback on gameplay, controls, difficulty, bugs, and other aspects of the game. Use this feedback to identify areas for improvement and iterate on your game design.

Publishing Your Game

ONCE YOU'RE SATISFIED with your game and confident in its quality, you can consider publishing it for others to play. There are various platforms and distribution channels available for publishing indie games, including online marketplaces, game portals, and social media platforms. Choose a platform that best suits your game and audience, and follow the guidelines for submitting your game for distribution.

Chapter 2: Drawing with Pygame

2.1 Basic Drawing: Shapes and Lines

DRAWING BASIC SHAPES and lines is one of the fundamental aspects of creating graphical applications with Pygame. Pygame provides functions for drawing various shapes, including rectangles, circles, polygons, and lines. In this section, we'll explore how to use these functions to draw basic shapes and lines on the screen.

Drawing Rectangles

RECTANGLES ARE ONE of the most commonly used shapes in game development. Pygame provides the pygame.draw.rect() function for drawing rectangles on the screen. This function takes several arguments, including the surface to draw on, the color of the rectangle, and a tuple specifying the position and size of the rectangle.

Drawing Circles

CIRCLES ARE ANOTHER commonly used shape in game development, especially for representing objects such as balls or coins. Pygame provides the pygame.draw.circle() function for drawing circles on the screen. Like pygame.draw.rect(), this function takes arguments specifying the surface to draw on, the color of the circle, and a tuple specifying the position and radius of the circle.

Drawing Lines

LINES ARE ESSENTIAL for creating paths, boundaries, and other geometric shapes in games. Pygame provides the pygame.draw.line() function for drawing lines on the screen. This function takes arguments specifying the surface to draw on, the color of the line, the starting and ending points of the line, and the line width.

Drawing Polygons

POLYGONS ARE VERSATILE shapes that can be used to create a wide variety of geometric shapes and patterns. Pygame provides the pygame.draw.polygon() function for drawing polygons on the screen. This function takes arguments specifying the surface to draw on, the color of the polygon, and a list of vertices defining the shape of the polygon.

Anti-aliasing

ANTI-ALIASING IS A technique used to smooth the edges of shapes and lines, reducing jaggedness and improving visual quality. Pygame provides support for anti-aliasing in its drawing functions by default, resulting in smoother and more visually appealing graphics. However, anti-aliasing can impact performance, so it's essential to consider the trade-offs when using it in your game.

Filling Shapes

IN ADDITION TO DRAWING outlines, Pygame allows you to fill shapes with color using the pygame.draw.rect() and pygame.draw.circle() functions. Simply specify a color value for the fill parameter to fill the shape with the specified color. This can be useful for creating solid shapes or highlighting areas of the screen.

Using Colors

COLORS PLAY A CRUCIAL role in game development, helping to differentiate objects, convey information, and create visual interest. Pygame represents colors using RGB (red, green, blue) values, with each component ranging from 0 to 255. You can specify colors using tuples (R, G, B) or use predefined color constants such as pygame.Color('red') or pygame.Color(255, 0, 0).

Drawing Text

IN ADDITION TO DRAWING shapes and lines, Pygame allows you to render text on the screen using the pygame.font.Font() and render() functions. You can create a font object using the pygame.font.Font() function, specify the text content and color, and render the text onto a surface using the render() function. This can be useful for displaying game scores, messages, and other textual information.

2.2 Working with Colors and Fill

WORKING WITH COLORS and fill is essential for creating visually appealing graphics in Pygame. Pygame provides various functions and techniques for specifying colors, filling shapes, and adding depth and realism to your game graphics. In this section, we'll explore how to work with colors and fill in Pygame.

Specifying Colors

PYGAME REPRESENTS COLORS using RGB (red, green, blue) values, with each component ranging from 0 to 255. You can specify colors using tuples (R, G, B) or use predefined color constants such as pygame.Color('red') or pygame.Color(255, 0, 0). Additionally, Pygame supports alpha values for specifying transparency, allowing you to create translucent or semi-transparent colors.

Color Blending and Mixing

COLOR BLENDING AND mixing are techniques used to create new colors by combining existing colors. Pygame provides functions for blending colors using various blending modes, including additive blending, subtractive blending, and alpha blending. These blending modes can be used to create effects such as shadows, highlights, gradients, and textures in your game graphics.

Filling Shapes with Color

IN PYGAME, YOU CAN fill shapes with color using the pygame.draw.rect() and pygame.draw.circle() functions. Simply specify a color value for the fill parameter to fill the shape with the specified color. This can be useful for creating solid shapes or highlighting areas of the screen. Additionally, Pygame provides the pygame.Surface.fill() method for filling entire surfaces with color.

Creating Gradients

GRADIENTS ARE SMOOTH transitions between two or more colors, often used to add depth and realism to game graphics. Pygame allows you to create gradients using custom drawing functions or by manipulating pixel values directly. You can create linear gradients, radial gradients, and other types of gradients to achieve various visual effects in your game.

Adding Shadows and Highlights

SHADOWS AND HIGHLIGHTS are essential for creating depth and realism in game graphics. Pygame provides techniques for adding shadows and highlights to objects by blending colors and adjusting brightness levels. You can simulate shadows and highlights using alpha blending, lighting effects, and other shading techniques to enhance the visual appeal of your game.

Using Textures and Patterns

TEXTURES AND PATTERNS are repeating visual elements used to add detail and complexity to game graphics. Pygame allows you to create textures and patterns by tiling small images or patterns across surfaces. You can use textures and patterns to simulate materials such as wood, metal, fabric, and stone, adding realism and visual interest to your game environments.

Applying Filters and Effects

FILTERS AND EFFECTS are post-processing techniques used to modify the appearance of game graphics. Pygame provides functions for applying filters and effects such as blur, sharpen, sepia, grayscale, and bloom to surfaces and sprites. These effects can be used to create artistic effects, simulate camera effects, and enhance the overall visual quality of your game.

Color Spaces and Models

UNDERSTANDING COLOR spaces and models is essential for working with colors in Pygame. Pygame supports various color spaces and models, including RGB, CMYK (cyan, magenta, yellow, black), HSL (hue, saturation, lightness), and HSV (hue, saturation, value). Each color space has its advantages and applications, depending on the requirements of your game graphics.

Color Management and Calibration

COLOR MANAGEMENT AND calibration are techniques used to ensure consistent and accurate color reproduction across different devices and platforms. Pygame provides functions for color management, including color profiles, color spaces, and gamma correction. Proper color management and calibration are essential for achieving the desired visual fidelity and accuracy in your game graphics.

2.3 Advanced Drawing Techniques

ADVANCED DRAWING TECHNIQUES in Pygame allow developers to create complex and visually stunning graphics for their games. These techniques go beyond basic shapes and lines, incorporating features such as gradients, transformations, and custom drawing functions. In this section, we'll explore some of the advanced drawing techniques available in Pygame.

Gradient Fills

GRADIENT FILLS ARE smooth transitions between two or more colors, often used to add depth and realism to game graphics. Pygame allows developers to create gradient fills using custom drawing functions or by manipulating pixel values directly. Gradients can be linear or radial and can be applied to shapes, surfaces, or entire screens.

Image Blending and Alpha Compositing

IMAGE BLENDING AND alpha compositing are techniques used to combine multiple images or surfaces together, allowing for complex visual effects. Pygame provides functions for blending images with different blending modes, including additive blending, subtractive blending, and alpha blending. These blending modes can be used to create effects such as transparency, shadows, and glows.

Texture Mapping

TEXTURE MAPPING IS a technique used to apply textures to surfaces or objects in a game. Pygame allows developers to load images as textures and map them onto surfaces using the pygame.transform.scale() and pygame.transform.rotate() functions.

Texture mapping can be used to create realistic-looking objects, terrain, and environments in games.

Anti-aliasing and Smoothing

ANTI-ALIASING IS A technique used to smooth the edges of shapes and lines, reducing jaggedness and improving visual quality. Pygame provides support for anti-aliasing in its drawing functions by default, resulting in smoother and more visually appealing graphics. Developers can control the level of anti-aliasing using parameters such as line width and surface flags.

Transformations and Translations

TRANSFORMATIONS AND translations allow developers to manipulate the position, size, rotation, and scale of objects in a game. Pygame provides functions for applying transformations and translations to surfaces and sprites, including scaling, rotating, flipping, and shearing. These transformations can be used to create dynamic animations and effects in games.

Custom Drawing Functions

CUSTOM DRAWING FUNCTIONS allow developers to create their own drawing routines for generating complex shapes, patterns, and effects. Pygame provides a flexible drawing API that allows developers to define custom shapes, lines, and fills using mathematical equations, algorithms, and procedural generation techniques. Custom drawing functions can be used to create unique visual styles and effects in games.

Hardware Acceleration

HARDWARE ACCELERATION is a technique used to offload graphics processing tasks to the GPU (graphics processing unit), resulting in faster and more efficient rendering. Pygame provides support for hardware acceleration through its integration with hardware-accelerated graphics APIs such as OpenGL and DirectX. Developers can take advantage of hardware acceleration to render complex scenes with high frame rates and smooth animations.

Vector Graphics and SVG Support

VECTOR GRAPHICS ARE resolution-independent graphics that are defined using mathematical equations rather than pixels. Pygame provides support for vector graphics through its integration with the SVG (Scalable Vector Graphics) format. Developers can load and render SVG files using the pygame_svg library, allowing for scalable and high-quality graphics in their games.

Advanced Rendering Techniques

ADVANCED RENDERING techniques such as ray tracing, ambient occlusion, and global illumination can be used to create realistic lighting and shading effects in games. While Pygame does not natively support these techniques, developers can implement them using custom shaders and rendering pipelines in combination with Pygame's drawing and rendering functions. Advanced rendering techniques can add a level of realism and immersion to games that is not possible with traditional rendering methods.

2.4 Animating Drawn Objects

ANIMATING DRAWN OBJECTS is a crucial aspect of game development that brings life and dynamism to game graphics. Pygame provides various techniques and methods for animating drawn objects, including sprite animation, frame-based animation, and procedural animation. In this section, we'll explore how to animate drawn objects in Pygame.

Animating drawn objects in Pygame often involves updating the position, rotation, scale, or appearance of objects over time to create the illusion of motion. This can be achieved by modifying the properties of objects in each frame of the game loop based on predefined animation sequences or algorithms.

Sprite Animation

SPRITE ANIMATION IS a popular technique for animating game characters, objects, and effects in Pygame. It involves displaying a sequence of images, known as frames, in rapid succession to create the illusion of motion. Pygame provides the pygame.sprite.Sprite class for representing animated objects and the pygame.sprite.Group class for managing collections of sprites.

Frame-Based Animation

FRAME-BASED ANIMATION is another common technique for animating drawn objects in Pygame. It involves defining a series of frames, each representing a different state or pose of the object, and displaying these frames sequentially to create the animation. Pygame provides functions for loading and displaying images, making it easy to implement frame-based animation in your game.

Keyframe Animation

KEYFRAME ANIMATION is a technique for animating drawn objects by specifying keyframes, or key positions, at specific points in time and interpolating between these keyframes to generate the animation. Pygame does not provide built-in support for keyframe animation, but developers can implement it using custom animation systems or third-party libraries.

Procedural Animation

PROCEDURAL ANIMATION is a technique for animating drawn objects using algorithms, simulations, or mathematical equations rather than predefined animation sequences. Pygame provides support for procedural animation through its drawing and transformation functions, allowing developers to create dynamic and interactive animations using code.

Tweening and Interpolation

TWEENING AND INTERPOLATION are techniques used to generate smooth transitions between keyframes or states in an animation. Pygame provides support for tweening and interpolation through third-party libraries such as PyTweening, which allows developers to define easing functions and apply them to animation sequences to create more natural and visually appealing motion.

Physics-Based Animation

PHYSICS-BASED ANIMATION is a technique for animating drawn objects based on physical principles such as gravity, velocity, acceleration, and collision detection. Pygame provides support for physics-based animation through its integration with physics engines such as PyBox2D and Pymunk, allowing developers to create realistic and interactive simulations of physical objects in their games.

Particle Systems

PARTICLE SYSTEMS ARE a versatile technique for creating dynamic and realistic effects such as fire, smoke, explosions, and magical effects in games. Pygame provides support for particle systems through custom drawing functions and libraries such as PygameParticles, allowing developers to create complex and visually stunning effects with ease.

Timing and Synchronization

TIMING AND SYNCHRONIZATION are critical aspects of animation in Pygame, ensuring that animations play at the correct speed and timing relative to the game loop. Pygame provides functions for controlling the timing of animations, including pygame.time.Clock.tick() for controlling the frame rate and pygame.time.get_ticks() for measuring elapsed time.

Optimizing Animation Performance

OPTIMIZING ANIMATION performance is essential for ensuring smooth and responsive gameplay in Pygame. Developers can optimize animation performance by reducing the number of objects and effects being animated, simplifying the animation logic, using hardware acceleration, and profiling and optimizing code for better performance.

2.5 Drawing Text and Fonts

DRAWING TEXT AND USING fonts is an essential aspect of game development in Pygame, allowing developers to display information, messages, scores, and user interface elements on the screen. In this section, we'll explore how to draw text and use fonts in Pygame to enhance the visual presentation of games.

Drawing text in Pygame is straightforward using the pygame.font.Font() and render() functions. Developers can create a font object using the pygame.font.Font() function, specify the text content, font size, and color, and render the text onto a surface using the render() function.

Pygame provides support for loading and using TrueType fonts (.ttf) and other font formats, allowing developers to choose from a wide range of fonts for their games. Fonts can be loaded using the pygame.font.Font() function or by using predefined font constants such as pygame.font.SysFont().

Font rendering in Pygame supports anti-aliasing by default, resulting in smooth and visually appealing text on the screen. Developers can control the anti-aliasing level and other text rendering options using the antialias parameter of the render() function.

Text can be rendered onto any surface in Pygame, including the game window, sprites, and user interface elements. Developers can specify the position, alignment, and other properties of the rendered text using parameters such as position, center, right, bottom, and top.

Pygame provides support for text wrapping, allowing developers to automatically wrap long lines of text to fit within a specified width.

This can be useful for displaying paragraphs of text, messages, or other content that may exceed the width of the screen or window.

In addition to rendering static text, Pygame allows developers to create dynamic text effects such as scrolling text, typewriter text, and animated text. These effects can be achieved by updating the position, appearance, or content of text in each frame of the game loop.

Pygame provides functions for measuring the size of rendered text, allowing developers to calculate the width and height of text before rendering it onto a surface. This can be useful for layout and positioning text elements within the game interface.

Font management is an important aspect of working with text in Pygame, ensuring that fonts are loaded, cached, and unloaded efficiently to minimize memory usage and performance overhead. Developers can use dictionaries or data structures to manage fonts and avoid reloading fonts unnecessarily.

Pygame supports Unicode text rendering, allowing developers to display text in multiple languages, character sets, and writing systems. Developers can specify Unicode strings as text content and render them onto surfaces using the render() function.

Text rendering performance can be optimized in Pygame by pre-rendering text onto surfaces and caching the rendered text for reuse. This can reduce the overhead of rendering text in each frame of the game loop and improve overall performance, especially for dynamic or frequently changing text.

Font rendering in Pygame can be customized using font styles, effects, and decorations such as bold, italic, underline, and strikeout. Developers can specify these properties when creating font objects using the pygame.font.Font() function or by applying text formatting options to rendered text surfaces.

Pygame provides support for text input and text editing, allowing developers to create text input fields, text boxes, and other user interface elements that accept user input. Developers can use the pygame.event module to handle keyboard events and update text content dynamically in response to user input.

Text rendering in Pygame can be extended and enhanced using third-party libraries and tools such as pygame_textinput, pygame_gui, and pytweener. These libraries provide additional functionality and features for working with text, including advanced text layout, formatting, and styling options.

Font rendering performance can be affected by factors such as the number of fonts, font sizes, and text rendering options used in a game. Developers can optimize font rendering performance by minimizing the number of unique fonts and font sizes used, reducing the complexity of text rendering operations, and profiling and optimizing font rendering code for better performance.

Overall, text rendering and font management in Pygame provide developers with powerful tools and techniques for displaying text and fonts in their games. By leveraging these features effectively, developers can create immersive, visually appealing, and user-friendly game interfaces that enhance the overall gaming experience.

Chapter 3: Handling Events

3.1 Understanding Event Handling in Pygame

EVENT HANDLING IS A fundamental aspect of game development in Pygame, allowing developers to respond to user input, system events, and other interactions in their games. In this section, we'll explore how event handling works in Pygame and how developers can use it to create interactive and responsive games.

Pygame uses an event-driven architecture, where events are generated by the user, system, or other sources and are then processed by the game loop. Events represent various types of interactions, such as keyboard presses, mouse movements, window events, and custom events created by the game developer.

The main event loop in Pygame is responsible for continuously checking for new events, processing them, and updating the game state accordingly. This loop typically runs in the main game loop alongside other game logic and rendering tasks, ensuring that the game remains responsive to user input and other events.

Pygame provides the pygame.event.get() function for retrieving a list of all pending events from the event queue. Developers can iterate over this list and process each event individually, checking its type and attributes to determine the appropriate response.

Common event types in Pygame include pygame.QUIT for quitting the game, pygame.KEYDOWN and pygame.KEYUP for keyboard input, pygame.MOUSEBUTTONDOWN and pygame.MOUSEBUTTONUP for mouse input, pygame.MOUSEMOTION for mouse movement, and pygame.USEREVENT for custom events created by the game developer.

Keyboard events in Pygame provide information about which keys were pressed or released, allowing developers to respond to specific key presses or combinations of keys. This can be useful for implementing player controls, menu navigation, and other interactions that rely on keyboard input.

Mouse events in Pygame provide information about mouse button presses, releases, and movements, including the position of the mouse cursor. Developers can use mouse events to implement features such as clicking on buttons, dragging objects, and selecting items in the game world.

Window events in Pygame provide information about changes to the game window, such as resizing, minimizing, maximizing, and closing the window. Developers can use window events to implement features such as adjusting the game resolution, handling fullscreen mode, and confirming exit prompts.

Custom events in Pygame allow developers to define their own event types and dispatch them to the event queue for processing. This can be useful for implementing game-specific events, such as triggering cutscenes, spawning enemies, or advancing the game state based on certain conditions.

Event handling in Pygame is typically integrated into the main game loop, where events are retrieved, processed, and dispatched in each iteration of the loop. Developers can use conditional statements, switch cases, or event handlers to respond to different types of events and execute corresponding actions or functions.

Event handling in Pygame can be extended and customized using event filters, which allow developers to intercept and modify events before they are added to the event queue. Event filters can be used to implement input validation, event routing, and other advanced event processing logic in Pygame.

Overall, event handling is a crucial aspect of game development in Pygame, enabling developers to create interactive and engaging experiences for players. By understanding how event handling works and how to use it effectively, developers can implement complex interactions, user interfaces, and game mechanics in their games with ease.

3.2 Managing Keyboard Inputs

MANAGING KEYBOARD INPUTS is a critical aspect of game development in Pygame, allowing developers to implement player controls, menu navigation, and other interactions that rely on keyboard input. In this section, we'll explore how to manage keyboard inputs in Pygame and how developers can use them effectively in their games.

Pygame provides functions for detecting and handling keyboard inputs, including key presses, key releases, and key combinations. Developers can use these functions to respond to specific keys being pressed or released and execute corresponding actions or functions in their games.

The main function for managing keyboard inputs in Pygame is pygame.event.get(), which retrieves a list of all pending events from the event queue. Developers can iterate over this list and check for keyboard events using conditional statements or event handlers.

Keyboard events in Pygame are represented by the pygame.KEYDOWN and pygame.KEYUP event types, which indicate when a key is pressed or released, respectively. Each keyboard event contains information about which key was pressed or released, allowing developers to respond to specific keys or key combinations.

To detect individual key presses, developers can use the event.key attribute of keyboard events, which contains the key code of the pressed key. Key codes are represented by constants such as pygame.K_LEFT, pygame.K_RIGHT, pygame.K_UP, pygame.K_DOWN for arrow keys, and pygame.K_SPACE, pygame.K_RETURN, pygame.K_ESCAPE for spacebar, enter, and escape keys, respectively.

Developers can use conditional statements or switch cases to check for specific key codes and execute corresponding actions or functions in response to key presses. This can be useful for implementing player movement, weapon selection, menu navigation, and other gameplay mechanics that rely on keyboard input.

To detect key combinations, developers can use boolean variables or flags to keep track of the state of individual keys and check for combinations of keys being pressed simultaneously. For example, developers can use flags such as left_key_pressed, right_key_pressed, up_key_pressed, down_key_pressed to detect combinations of arrow keys being pressed together.

Pygame provides support for key repetition, allowing developers to detect when a key is held down for an extended period and trigger repeated key presses at regular intervals. This can be useful for implementing continuous actions such as scrolling, firing weapons, or accelerating movement in response to prolonged key presses.

In addition to detecting individual key presses, Pygame allows developers to create custom key bindings and keyboard shortcuts for specific actions or functions in their games. This can be achieved by mapping key codes to action names or function calls using dictionaries or data structures and processing keyboard events accordingly.

Keyboard input in Pygame can be integrated into the main game loop, where keyboard events are retrieved, processed, and dispatched in each iteration of the loop. Developers can use event handlers, callbacks, or dedicated input processing functions to manage keyboard inputs efficiently and ensure responsive gameplay.

Overall, managing keyboard inputs in Pygame is essential for creating interactive and engaging games that respond to player actions in real-time. By understanding how to detect and handle keyboard events effectively, developers can implement complex interactions, controls, and gameplay mechanics that enhance the overall gaming experience.

3.3 Handling Mouse Events

HANDLING MOUSE EVENTS is a crucial aspect of game development in Pygame, allowing developers to implement various interactions such as clicking on buttons, dragging objects, and selecting items in the game world. In this section, we'll explore how to handle mouse events in Pygame and how developers can use them effectively in their games.

Pygame provides functions for detecting and handling mouse events, including mouse button presses, releases, and movements. Developers can use these functions to respond to user interactions with the mouse and execute corresponding actions or functions in their games.

The main function for handling mouse events in Pygame is pygame.event.get(), which retrieves a list of all pending events from the event queue. Developers can iterate over this list and check for mouse events using conditional statements or event handlers.

Mouse events in Pygame are represented by event types such as pygame.MOUSEBUTTONDOWN, pygame.MOUSEBUTTONUP, and pygame.MOUSEMOTION, which indicate when a mouse button is pressed, released, or when the mouse is moved, respectively. Each mouse event contains information about the position of the mouse cursor and which mouse button was pressed or released.

To detect mouse button presses and releases, developers can use the event.type attribute of mouse events to check for specific event types such as pygame.MOUSEBUTTONDOWN and pygame.MOUSEBUTTONUP. They can also use the event.button attribute to determine which mouse button was pressed or released, such as the left, right, or middle mouse button.

Developers can use conditional statements or switch cases to check for specific mouse button presses or releases and execute corresponding actions or functions in response to user interactions. This can be useful for implementing features such as clicking on buttons, shooting projectiles, and interacting with objects in the game world.

To detect mouse movements, developers can use the pygame.MOUSEMOTION event type, which indicates when the mouse cursor is moved. Mouse motion events contain information about the position of the mouse cursor and the change in position since the last event, allowing developers to track the movement of the mouse and update the game state accordingly.

Mouse input in Pygame can be integrated into the main game loop, where mouse events are retrieved, processed, and dispatched in each iteration of the loop. Developers can use event handlers, callbacks, or dedicated input processing functions to manage mouse events efficiently and ensure responsive gameplay.

Pygame provides support for mouse position relative to the game window or screen coordinates, allowing developers to determine the position of the mouse cursor within the game world or user interface elements. This can be useful for implementing features such as selecting objects, moving the camera, and navigating menus.

In addition to detecting mouse events, Pygame allows developers to create custom mouse cursors and change the appearance of the mouse cursor based on different states or interactions in the game. This can be achieved using the pygame.mouse.set_cursor() function to set a custom cursor image or cursor hotspot.

Mouse input in Pygame can be extended and customized using third-party libraries and tools such as pygame_gui, which provides additional functionality and features for working with mouse events, including mouse-driven user interfaces, buttons, sliders, and interactive elements.

Overall, handling mouse events in Pygame is essential for creating interactive and engaging games that respond to user interactions with the mouse. By understanding how to detect and handle mouse events effectively, developers can implement complex interactions, controls, and gameplay mechanics that enhance the overall gaming experience.

3.4 Creating Custom Events

CREATING CUSTOM EVENTS is a powerful feature of Pygame that allows developers to define their own event types and dispatch them to the event queue for processing. In this section, we'll explore how to create custom events in Pygame and how developers can use them effectively in their games.

Custom events in Pygame are represented by user-defined event types, which can be any integer value greater than or equal to pygame.USEREVENT. Developers can define custom event types using integer constants or enumeration values to represent different types of events in their games.

To create a custom event in Pygame, developers can use the pygame.event.Event() constructor to create an event object with a specified type and optional attributes. The event type should be a unique integer value greater than or equal to pygame.USEREVENT, and the attributes can be any data type or value that provides additional information about the event.

Once a custom event object is created, developers can dispatch it to the event queue using the pygame.event.post() function, which adds the event to the end of the event queue for processing by the main event loop. Developers can specify the custom event object as an argument to the pygame.event.post() function to dispatch it to the event queue.

To handle custom events in the main event loop, developers can retrieve custom events from the event queue using the pygame.event.get() function and process them using conditional statements or event handlers. Developers can check the type of each event object to determine if it is a custom event and execute corresponding actions or functions based on the event type.

Custom events can be used for various purposes in Pygame, such as triggering cutscenes, spawning enemies, advancing the game state, and communicating between different parts of the game. Developers can define custom event types for specific game events or interactions and dispatch them to the event queue as needed.

In addition to dispatching custom events directly from within the game code, developers can also use event scheduling mechanisms such as timers, delays, and timeouts to automatically dispatch events at specific points in time. This can be useful for implementing timed events, animations, and scripted sequences in games.

Pygame provides support for event filtering, which allows developers to intercept and modify events before they are added to the event queue. Event filters can be used to preprocess events, perform input validation, or route events to different parts of the game based on specific criteria.

Event filtering in Pygame is achieved by registering event filter functions using the pygame.event.set_allowed() function, which specifies the types of events that should be allowed to pass through the filter. Developers can define custom event filter functions that inspect incoming events and modify them or discard them based on specific conditions.

Overall, creating custom events in Pygame is a versatile and powerful feature that allows developers to extend and customize the event handling system to suit their specific game requirements. By defining custom event types, dispatching them to the event queue, and handling them in the main event loop, developers can implement complex interactions, scripted sequences, and game mechanics that enhance the overall gaming experience.

3.5 Designing an Event-Driven Game Structure

DESIGNING AN EVENT-driven game structure is a fundamental aspect of game development in Pygame, allowing developers to create flexible, modular, and scalable game architectures that respond to user input, system events, and other interactions. In this section, we'll explore how to design an event-driven game structure in Pygame and how developers can use it effectively in their games.

An event-driven game structure in Pygame is based on the principle of event-driven programming, where events are used to trigger actions or functions in response to specific interactions or conditions. Events can represent various types of interactions, such as keyboard inputs, mouse clicks, collisions, timers, and custom game events created by the developer.

The main components of an event-driven game structure in Pygame include the event loop, event handlers, event listeners, and game objects that respond to events. The event loop continuously checks for new events, processes them, and dispatches them to event handlers or listeners for further processing.

Event handlers are functions or methods that are responsible for processing specific types of events and executing corresponding actions or functions in response. Event handlers can be defined for built-in event types such as keyboard inputs, mouse clicks, and collisions, as well as for custom event types created by the developer.

Event listeners are objects or components that listen for specific types of events and respond to them by executing predefined actions or functions. Event listeners can be attached to game objects, user interface elements, or other entities in the game world and can be used to implement interactions, behaviors, and game mechanics that rely on events.

The event loop in Pygame typically runs in the main game loop alongside other game logic and rendering tasks, ensuring that the game remains responsive to user input and other events. Developers can use conditional statements, switch cases, or event-driven architectures such as finite state machines to manage the flow of the game and respond to different types of events.

One common approach to designing an event-driven game structure in Pygame is to use a component-based architecture, where game objects are composed of multiple components that encapsulate different aspects of their behavior and functionality. Each component can have its own event handlers and listeners, allowing game objects to respond to events independently and interact with each other in a modular and extensible way.

Another approach to designing an event-driven game structure in Pygame is to use an entity-component system (ECS), where game entities are composed of multiple components that define their behavior, properties, and interactions. Entities can emit events, listen for events, and respond to events using event handlers and listeners, allowing for flexible and dynamic game architectures.

Event-driven game structures in Pygame can be extended and customized using third-party libraries, frameworks, and tools that provide additional functionality and features for event handling, such as pygame_gui, which provides a user interface toolkit with built-in event handling capabilities, or Pygame's built-in event scheduling mechanisms for timers, delays, and timeouts.

Overall, designing an event-driven game structure in Pygame is essential for creating flexible, modular, and scalable game architectures that respond to user input, system events, and other interactions. By using event-driven programming techniques, developers can create immersive, interactive, and engaging games that provide a rich and dynamic gameplay experience for players.

Chapter 4: Game Sprites and Images

4.1 Introduction to Sprites in Pygame

SPRITES ARE A FUNDAMENTAL concept in game development, representing movable objects or characters within the game world. In Pygame, sprites are typically used to represent characters, enemies, obstacles, projectiles, and other interactive elements that can be manipulated and displayed on the screen.

The pygame.sprite.Sprite class is the base class for all sprites in Pygame, providing common methods and attributes for managing sprites, such as position, velocity, collision detection, and rendering. Developers can create custom sprite classes by subclassing pygame.sprite.Sprite and adding additional attributes and methods specific to their game objects.

Sprites in Pygame are typically rendered onto the game screen using images or surfaces, which are loaded from image files or created dynamically using Pygame's drawing functions. Images can be loaded using the pygame.image.load() function, which returns a Surface object representing the image data.

Once an image is loaded, developers can create sprite objects using the pygame.sprite.Sprite class or custom sprite classes derived from it. Sprites can be positioned, rotated, scaled, and manipulated using Pygame's transformation functions, allowing for dynamic and interactive animations.

Pygame provides support for sprite groups, which are collections of sprites that can be updated and rendered together as a single unit. Sprite groups allow developers to efficiently manage large numbers of sprites, perform collision detection, and implement other group-based operations.

Sprite groups in Pygame are represented by the pygame.sprite.Group class, which provides methods for adding and removing sprites, updating sprite positions and states, and rendering sprites onto the game screen. Developers can create multiple sprite groups to organize sprites into logical categories or layers within the game world.

Collision detection is a common task in game development, and Pygame provides built-in support for detecting collisions between sprites using the pygame.sprite.spritecollide() function. This function checks for collisions between a sprite and a group of sprites and returns a list of sprites that intersect with the given sprite.

Developers can define custom collision detection logic by subclassing the pygame.sprite.Sprite class and implementing the collide_rect() or collide_mask() methods to define the collision boundaries of sprites. These methods can be overridden to provide custom collision detection behavior based on the shape and properties of sprites.

Pygame also provides support for sprite animation, allowing developers to create dynamic and engaging animations for sprites using sequences of images or frames. Sprites can be animated by changing their image data or sprite attributes over time, creating the illusion of movement, action, and interaction.

Sprite animation in Pygame can be achieved using techniques such as frame-based animation, where sprites are rendered using a sequence of images, and interpolation-based animation, where sprites are smoothly transitioned between different states or poses using mathematical functions.

In addition to traditional 2D sprites, Pygame also provides support for sprite-based particle systems, which allow developers to create dynamic and realistic effects such as explosions, fire, smoke, and rain. Particle systems can be implemented using sprites to represent individual particles and applying physics-based behaviors to simulate their movement and interaction.

Overall, sprites are a versatile and powerful tool for game development in Pygame, providing a flexible and efficient way to create interactive, animated, and visually appealing game objects. By understanding how to work with sprites and sprite-based systems effectively, developers can create immersive, engaging, and polished games that captivate players and deliver memorable gaming experiences.

4.2 Loading and Displaying Images

LOADING AND DISPLAYING images is a fundamental task in game development, allowing developers to render graphics, backgrounds, characters, and other visual elements onto the game screen. In Pygame, images are typically loaded from image files and displayed using surface objects, providing a flexible and efficient way to create visually appealing games.

Pygame provides the pygame.image.load() function for loading images from image files in various formats, such as PNG, JPEG, BMP, and GIF. This function returns a surface object representing the image data, which can then be manipulated, transformed, and rendered onto the game screen.

Once an image is loaded, developers can use Pygame's surface manipulation functions to transform and manipulate the image data as needed. Surface objects can be resized, rotated, flipped, cropped, and blended using Pygame's transformation and blending functions, allowing for dynamic and interactive graphics rendering.

To display an image onto the game screen, developers can use Pygame's blitting functions, such as pygame.Surface.blit(), which blits (copies) the pixels from one surface onto another surface. This function takes the source surface (the image to be displayed) and the destination surface (the screen or another surface) as arguments, as well as optional parameters for specifying the position, scale, rotation, and blending mode of the blitted image.

Images can be displayed at specific positions on the game screen by specifying the coordinates of the top-left corner of the image relative to the destination surface. Developers can use Pygame's coordinate system, where the origin (0,0) is located at the top-left corner of the screen, and positive x-coordinates extend to the right, while positive y-coordinates extend downward.

Pygame provides support for transparency and alpha blending, allowing developers to create images with transparent or semi-transparent regions that blend seamlessly with the background. Surface objects can be created with an alpha channel (an additional channel for storing transparency information), and images can be blitted onto the screen using alpha blending to achieve smooth, anti-aliased edges and transparent effects.

To optimize image loading and rendering performance, developers can use techniques such as image caching, preloading, and sprite sheets. Image caching involves loading images into memory once and reusing them throughout the game, reducing the overhead of loading images from disk repeatedly. Preloading involves loading images into memory before they are needed, reducing the delay when displaying images for the first time. Sprite sheets are large images that contain multiple smaller images (sprites), allowing developers to load and render multiple sprites with a single blit operation, reducing the number of surface manipulations and improving rendering performance.

Pygame provides support for hardware acceleration and hardware-accelerated rendering, allowing developers to take advantage of the underlying hardware capabilities of the graphics processing unit (GPU) for faster and more efficient image loading and rendering. Hardware acceleration can be enabled using Pygame's display mode functions, such as pygame.display.set_mode(), which allows developers to create hardware-accelerated display surfaces for rendering images onto the screen.

In addition to loading images from files, developers can also create images dynamically using Pygame's drawing functions, such as pygame.draw.rect(), pygame.draw.circle(), pygame.draw.line(), and pygame.draw.polygon(). These functions allow developers to create geometric shapes, lines, and patterns directly onto surface objects, providing a flexible and efficient way to generate dynamic graphics and visual effects in games.

Overall, loading and displaying images in Pygame is a fundamental task that is essential for creating visually appealing and immersive games. By understanding how to load, manipulate, and render images effectively, developers can create polished and professional-looking games that captivate players and deliver memorable gaming experiences.

4.3 Transforming and Animating Sprites

TRANSFORMING AND ANIMATING sprites are essential aspects of game development, allowing developers to create dynamic and engaging visuals that bring their games to life. In Pygame, sprites can be transformed using various techniques, such as rotation, scaling, flipping, and translation, while animation involves changing the appearance of sprites over time to create the illusion of movement and action.

Rotation is a common transformation applied to sprites in games, allowing developers to rotate sprites around their center point or a specified pivot point. Pygame provides the pygame.transform.rotate() function for rotating surface objects, which takes the source surface (the sprite) and the angle of rotation as arguments and returns a new surface object with the rotated image data.

Scaling is another transformation used to resize sprites in games, allowing developers to make sprites larger or smaller to fit different resolutions, aspect ratios, or display sizes. Pygame provides the pygame.transform.scale() function for scaling surface objects, which takes the source surface (the sprite) and the desired width and height as arguments and returns a new surface object with the scaled image data.

Flipping is a transformation used to mirror or flip sprites horizontally or vertically, allowing developers to create mirrored or flipped versions of sprites for visual variety or gameplay mechanics. Pygame provides the pygame.transform.flip() function for flipping surface objects, which takes the source surface (the sprite) and boolean flags for horizontal and vertical flipping as arguments and returns a new surface object with the flipped image data.

Translation, or movement, is a transformation used to change the position of sprites in the game world, allowing developers to animate sprites by moving them along a path or trajectory. Pygame provides support for sprite movement using sprite attributes such as position (x, y coordinates), velocity (speed and direction), and acceleration (rate of change of velocity), allowing developers to implement smooth and realistic sprite motion.

Animation involves changing the appearance of sprites over time by displaying a sequence of images or frames at regular intervals, creating the illusion of movement, action, and interaction. Pygame provides support for sprite animation using techniques such as frame-based animation and interpolation-based animation, allowing developers to create dynamic and engaging animations for sprites.

Frame-based animation involves displaying a sequence of images or frames in rapid succession, creating the illusion of movement and action. Pygame provides the pygame.time.Clock() class and the tick() method for controlling the frame rate of the game and updating sprite animations at regular intervals, ensuring smooth and consistent animation playback.

Interpolation-based animation involves smoothly transitioning sprites between different states or poses using mathematical functions, such as linear interpolation (lerp), cubic interpolation (cubic spline), or Bezier interpolation (Bezier curve). Pygame provides support for interpolation-based animation using techniques such as tweening libraries or custom animation functions, allowing developers to create fluid and natural-looking animations for sprites.

In addition to transforming and animating individual sprites, Pygame provides support for sprite groups and sprite-based systems, allowing developers to manage and animate multiple sprites simultaneously. Sprite groups allow developers to update and render multiple sprites as a single unit, improving performance and reducing code complexity.

Overall, transforming and animating sprites in Pygame is a fundamental aspect of game development that allows developers to create dynamic and immersive games. By understanding how to apply transformations, create animations, and manage sprite-based systems effectively, developers can create visually appealing and engaging games that captivate players and deliver memorable gaming experiences.

4.4 Sprite Collision Detection

SPRITE COLLISION DETECTION is a crucial aspect of game development, allowing developers to detect when sprites intersect or overlap with each other in the game world. In Pygame, sprite collision detection is commonly used for implementing gameplay mechanics such as player-enemy collisions, object interactions, and environmental hazards.

Pygame provides built-in support for sprite collision detection using the pygame.sprite.spritecollide() function, which checks for collisions between a sprite and a group of sprites and returns a list of sprites that intersect with the given sprite. This function takes the source sprite, the target sprite group, and an optional boolean flag for whether to remove collided sprites from the group as arguments.

Collision detection in Pygame is based on rectangular bounding boxes, where each sprite is enclosed within a rectangle that represents its collision boundaries. The pygame.sprite.spritecollide() function checks for collisions between the bounding boxes of sprites and returns a list of sprites that intersect with the given sprite, allowing developers to handle collisions and execute corresponding actions or functions in their games.

To implement custom collision detection logic, developers can subclass the pygame.sprite.Sprite class and override the collide_rect() or collide_mask() methods to define the collision boundaries of sprites. These methods can be customized to provide precise collision detection based on the shape and properties of sprites, such as irregular shapes, rotated sprites, or complex collision geometries.

In addition to rectangular bounding boxes, Pygame also provides support for pixel-perfect collision detection using masks, which represent the precise shape of sprites and allow for more accurate collision detection. The collide_mask() method of the pygame.sprite.Sprite class can be overridden to define custom collision masks for sprites, allowing developers to implement pixel-perfect collision detection based on the alpha channel of sprite images.

To optimize collision detection performance, developers can use techniques such as spatial partitioning, collision layers, and collision caching. Spatial partitioning involves dividing the game world into smaller regions or cells and organizing sprites into spatial data structures such as grids, trees, or lists, allowing for efficient collision detection between sprites that are close to each other in space.

Collision layers involve separating sprites into different layers or categories based on their collision properties or interactions, allowing developers to perform collision detection selectively between sprites on the same layer or between sprites on different layers. Collision caching involves precomputing and storing collision information between pairs of sprites, allowing for faster collision detection by avoiding redundant calculations.

Pygame also provides support for collision detection callbacks, which allow developers to register callback functions that are called automatically when collisions occur between sprites. Collision detection callbacks can be used to handle collisions and execute corresponding actions or functions in response, such as damaging players, destroying enemies, or triggering special effects.

Overall, sprite collision detection in Pygame is a fundamental aspect of game development that allows developers to implement complex interactions, gameplay mechanics, and environmental hazards. By understanding how to use built-in collision detection functions, implement custom collision detection logic, and optimize collision detection performance, developers can create immersive, challenging, and engaging games that captivate players and deliver memorable gaming experiences.

4.5 Organizing Sprites Using Groups

ORGANIZING SPRITES using groups is a common practice in Pygame game development, allowing developers to efficiently manage and manipulate multiple sprites as a single unit. Sprite groups provide a convenient way to update, render, and perform operations on groups of sprites, improving performance, reducing code complexity, and enhancing modularity in game development.

In Pygame, sprite groups are represented by the pygame.sprite.Group class, which provides methods and attributes for managing collections of sprites. Sprite groups can contain any number of sprites, which can be added, removed, updated, and rendered collectively using group-based operations.

To create a sprite group in Pygame, developers can simply instantiate an instance of the pygame.sprite.Group class, which initializes an empty group of sprites. Sprites can then be added to the group using the add() method, which takes one or more sprite objects as arguments and adds them to the group.

Sprite groups in Pygame provide several useful methods for managing sprites, such as update(), draw(), clear(), and empty(). The update() method updates the state of all sprites in the group by calling their update() methods, allowing developers to implement custom update logic for each sprite.

The draw() method renders all sprites in the group onto a specified surface, such as the game screen, by calling their draw() methods, which blit the sprite images onto the surface. This method allows developers to render multiple sprites with a single function call, improving rendering performance and reducing the number of surface manipulations.

The clear() method removes all sprites from the group, while the empty() method checks if the group is empty (i.e., contains no sprites). These methods can be used to manage the lifecycle of sprite groups and perform cleanup operations when sprites are no longer needed.

Sprite groups in Pygame can also be used for collision detection, allowing developers to check for collisions between sprites in the same group or between sprites in different groups. The pygame.sprite.spritecollide() function can be used to detect collisions between a sprite and a group of sprites, returning a list of collided sprites.

To improve performance and optimize collision detection, developers can organize sprites into separate collision groups based on their collision properties or interactions. Collision groups allow developers to selectively perform collision detection between specific groups of sprites, reducing the number of pairwise collision checks and improving performance.

In addition to collision detection, sprite groups can be used for other group-based operations, such as sprite management, rendering optimization, and gameplay mechanics. For example, developers can use sprite groups to implement sprite pooling, object pooling, or spatial partitioning for efficient sprite management and rendering.

Overall, organizing sprites using groups in Pygame is a powerful technique that allows developers to manage and manipulate multiple sprites efficiently in game development. By understanding how to use sprite groups effectively, developers can create modular, scalable, and performant games that provide a seamless and immersive gaming experience for players.

Chapter 5: Sound and Music

5.1 Loading and Playing Sound Effects

LOADING AND PLAYING sound effects is an important aspect of game development, adding auditory feedback and immersion to games. In Pygame, sound effects can be loaded from audio files and played using the pygame.mixer.Sound class, providing a simple and efficient way to incorporate sound into games.

To load a sound effect in Pygame, developers can use the pygame.mixer.Sound class constructor, passing the filename of the audio file as an argument. Pygame supports various audio formats, such as WAV, MP3, OGG, and FLAC, allowing developers to use a wide range of sound files for their games.

Once a sound effect is loaded, developers can play it using the play() method of the pygame.mixer.Sound class, which starts playing the sound effect from the beginning. The play() method can also take optional arguments for controlling the number of times the sound effect is played (looping), the volume level, and the fade-in and fade-out durations.

Pygame provides support for controlling the playback of sound effects, allowing developers to pause, resume, stop, and rewind sound effects as needed. The pause() and unpause() methods can be used to pause and resume the playback of sound effects, while the stop() method stops the playback and resets the sound effect to the beginning.

To control the volume level of sound effects, developers can use the set_volume() method of the pygame.mixer.Sound class, which takes a floating-point value between 0.0 (silent) and 1.0 (maximum volume) as an argument. This method allows developers to adjust the volume of sound effects dynamically during gameplay.

Pygame also provides support for fading sound effects in and out, allowing developers to create smooth transitions between different audio tracks or scenes. The fadeout() method of the pygame.mixer.Sound class can be used to fade out the volume of a sound effect over a specified duration, creating a gradual decrease in volume.

In addition to playing standalone sound effects, Pygame supports playing multiple sound effects simultaneously, allowing developers to create complex audio compositions and layered soundscapes. Sound effects can be played concurrently using separate instances of the pygame.mixer.Sound class, with each instance representing a different sound effect.

To manage multiple sound effects and control their playback, developers can use the pygame.mixer.Channel class, which represents a single audio channel for playing sound effects. Pygame provides a default set of audio channels, which can be accessed using the pygame.mixer.Channel class constructor or the pygame.mixer.get_channel() function.

By default, Pygame allocates a fixed number of audio channels for playing sound effects, typically ranging from 8 to 32 channels depending on the platform and hardware. Developers can adjust the number of audio channels and configure their properties using the pygame.mixer.set_num_channels() function, allowing for greater control over audio playback and resource management.

Overall, loading and playing sound effects in Pygame is a straightforward process that enhances the audiovisual experience of games. By understanding how to use the pygame.mixer.Sound class, control sound playback, adjust volume levels, and manage audio channels effectively, developers can create immersive, dynamic, and engaging games that captivate players and deliver memorable gaming experiences.

5.2 Working with Background Music

BACKGROUND MUSIC PLAYS a crucial role in setting the mood, atmosphere, and tone of games, enhancing the overall gaming experience for players. In Pygame, background music can be loaded from audio files and played using the pygame.mixer.music module, providing a simple and efficient way to incorporate music into games.

To load background music in Pygame, developers can use the pygame.mixer.music.load() function, passing the filename of the audio file as an argument. Pygame supports various audio formats for background music, such as WAV, MP3, OGG, and FLAC, allowing developers to use a wide range of music files for their games.

Once background music is loaded, developers can start playing it using the pygame.mixer.music.play() function, which starts playing the music from the beginning. The play() function can also take optional arguments for controlling the number of times the music is played (looping), the starting position, and the fade-in duration.

Pygame provides support for controlling the playback of background music, allowing developers to pause, resume, stop, rewind, and fade music as needed. The pygame.mixer.music.pause() and pygame.mixer.music.unpause() functions can be used to pause and resume the playback of music, while the stop() function stops the playback and resets the music to the beginning.

To control the volume level of background music, developers can use the pygame.mixer.music.set_volume() function, which takes a floating-point value between 0.0 (silent) and 1.0 (maximum volume) as an argument. This function allows developers to adjust the volume of background music dynamically during gameplay.

Pygame also provides support for fading background music in and out, allowing developers to create smooth transitions between different music tracks or scenes. The pygame.mixer.music.fadeout() function can be used to fade out the volume of background music over a specified duration, creating a gradual decrease in volume.

In addition to playing standalone music tracks, Pygame supports playing multiple music tracks sequentially or in a playlist format, allowing developers to create dynamic music compositions and playlists for different game events or scenes. Music tracks can be queued for playback using the pygame.mixer.music.queue() function, which adds a music track to the end of the music queue.

To manage multiple music tracks and control their playback, developers can use the pygame.mixer.music.get_busy() function to check if music is currently playing, the pygame.mixer.music.get_pos() function to get the current playback position, and the pygame.mixer.music.set_endevent() function to set an end-of-track event that is triggered when a music track finishes playing.

By leveraging the features and functions provided by the pygame.mixer.music module, developers can create immersive, dynamic, and interactive music experiences in their games. By understanding how to load music, control playback, adjust volume levels, and manage music tracks effectively, developers can create games with rich, engaging, and memorable soundscapes that captivate players and enhance the overall gaming experience.

5.3 Managing Sound Volumes and Playback

MANAGING SOUND VOLUMES and playback is essential for creating a balanced audio experience in games, ensuring that sound effects, background music, and other audio elements are heard clearly without overpowering each other or the overall gameplay experience. In Pygame, developers have various options for controlling sound volumes, adjusting playback parameters, and fine-tuning audio settings to achieve the desired audio balance and immersion in their games.

One of the key aspects of managing sound volumes in Pygame is controlling the volume levels of individual sound effects and background music. Pygame provides functions such as pygame.mixer.Sound.set_volume() and pygame.mixer.music.set_volume() to adjust the volume levels of sound effects and background music, respectively. These functions take floating-point values between 0.0 (silent) and 1.0 (maximum volume) as arguments, allowing developers to dynamically adjust the volume levels of audio elements during gameplay based on player preferences or game events.

In addition to adjusting volume levels, Pygame also provides support for controlling the overall playback speed of sound effects and background music. The pygame.mixer.Sound.set_speed() function can be used to adjust the playback speed of sound effects, while the pygame.mixer.music.set_speed() function can be used to adjust the playback speed of background music. These functions take floating-point values representing playback speed multipliers as arguments, allowing developers to create special effects, slow-motion sequences, or fast-paced gameplay dynamics by altering the playback speed of audio elements.

Pygame also provides support for controlling the stereo panning of sound effects and background music, allowing developers to position audio elements in the virtual sound space and create spatial audio effects. The pygame.mixer.Sound.set_pan() function can be used to adjust the stereo panning of sound effects, while the pygame.mixer.music.set_pan() function can be used to adjust the stereo panning of background music. These functions take integer values between -1 (full left) and 1 (full right) as arguments, allowing developers to pan audio elements between the left and right stereo channels to create immersive and directional audio experiences.

Another aspect of managing sound volumes and playback in Pygame is controlling the spatial attenuation of sound effects, which simulates the decrease in volume as sound sources move farther away from the listener in the virtual game world. Pygame provides support for spatial attenuation using the pygame.mixer.Sound.set_volume() function and the pygame.mixer.Sound.get_distance() function, which allow developers to adjust the volume levels of sound effects based on their distance from the listener and the attenuation properties specified in the sound effect's audio file.

Additionally, Pygame provides functions such as pygame.mixer.fadeout() and pygame.mixer.music.fadeout() to create smooth fade-out effects for sound effects and background music, respectively. These functions take an integer value representing the fade-out duration in milliseconds as an argument, gradually decreasing the volume levels of audio elements over the specified duration to create a gradual decrease in volume and a seamless transition between different audio tracks or scenes.

Overall, managing sound volumes and playback in Pygame is a versatile and flexible process that allows developers to create immersive, dynamic, and interactive audio experiences in their games. By understanding how to adjust volume levels, control playback speed and stereo panning, simulate spatial attenuation, and create fade-out effects, developers can create games with rich, engaging, and memorable audio landscapes that enhance the overall gaming experience and captivate players.

5.4 Synchronizing Sounds with Game Events

SYNCHRONIZING SOUNDS with game events is essential for creating immersive and responsive audio experiences in games, where sound effects, background music, and other audio elements are triggered dynamically in response to player actions, game events, and environmental conditions. In Pygame, developers have various options for synchronizing sounds with game events, allowing them to create dynamic audio compositions, synchronize sound effects with gameplay mechanics, and enhance the overall audiovisual experience of their games.

One of the key aspects of synchronizing sounds with game events in Pygame is triggering sound effects in response to specific game events, such as player actions, object interactions, or environmental changes. Pygame provides functions such as pygame.mixer.Sound.play() and pygame.mixer.music.play() to play sound effects and background music, respectively, allowing developers to trigger audio playback in response to game events using event handlers, game loops, or other game logic.

In addition to triggering sounds manually, Pygame also provides support for scheduling sound playback at specific times or intervals using the pygame.mixer.Sound.play() function with optional arguments for controlling the starting position, number of times played, and delay before playback. This allows developers to synchronize sound effects with scripted events, animations, or timed sequences in their games, creating dynamic and interactive audio experiences that respond to player input and game state changes.

Another aspect of synchronizing sounds with game events in Pygame is controlling the timing and duration of sound playback to create rhythmic patterns, musical motifs, or audio cues that enhance the gameplay experience. Pygame provides functions such as pygame.mixer.Sound.set_endevent() and pygame.mixer.music.set_endevent() to set end-of-track events that are triggered when a sound effect or background music finishes playing, allowing developers to synchronize sound playback with game events, transitions, or animations.

Pygame also provides support for synchronizing sounds with visual effects, animations, or game state changes using event-driven programming techniques, such as event listeners, callbacks, or custom event handlers. Developers can use the pygame.event.Event class to create custom events and trigger sound playback in response to specific events, allowing for seamless integration of audio and visual elements in games and enhancing the overall immersion and interactivity of the gaming experience.

Additionally, Pygame provides support for synchronizing sounds with real-time gameplay mechanics, such as physics simulations, collision detection, or artificial intelligence algorithms. Developers can use game loops, update functions, or state machines to synchronize sound playback with game events and actions, allowing for dynamic and responsive audio feedback that reflects the state of the game world and engages players on a deeper level.

Overall, synchronizing sounds with game events in Pygame is a versatile and powerful technique that allows developers to create immersive, dynamic, and interactive audio experiences in their games. By understanding how to trigger sound effects, schedule sound playback, control timing and duration, synchronize audio and visual elements, and integrate audio feedback with gameplay mechanics, developers can create games with rich, engaging, and memorable audio landscapes that captivate players and enhance the overall gaming experience.

5.5 Advanced Audio Techniques in Pygame

ADVANCED AUDIO TECHNIQUES in Pygame encompass a range of features and strategies for enhancing the audio experience in games, including spatial audio effects, dynamic mixing, procedural audio generation, and real-time audio processing. These techniques allow developers to create immersive, interactive, and responsive audio environments that complement the gameplay experience and engage players on a deeper level.

One advanced audio technique in Pygame is spatial audio, which simulates the three-dimensional positioning of sound sources in the virtual game world, creating a sense of depth, directionality, and immersion for players. Pygame provides support for spatial audio effects using the pygame.mixer.Sound.set_volume() function and the pygame.mixer.Sound.set_pan() function, which allow developers to adjust the volume levels and stereo panning of sound effects based on their position relative to the listener.

Another advanced audio technique in Pygame is dynamic mixing, which involves adjusting the volume levels, playback speed, and other audio properties of sound effects and background music in real time based on game events, player actions, and environmental conditions. Pygame provides functions such as pygame.mixer.Sound.set_volume() and pygame.mixer.Sound.set_speed() to dynamically adjust the volume levels and playback speed of sound effects, allowing developers to create adaptive audio experiences that respond to changes in the game world.

Procedural audio generation is another advanced audio technique in Pygame, which involves generating sound effects, background music, and other audio elements algorithmically in real time based on mathematical models, procedural algorithms, or user-defined parameters. Pygame provides support for procedural audio generation using the pygame.mixer.Sound class constructor and the pygame.mixer.Sound.play() function, allowing developers to generate and play custom sound effects on the fly.

Real-time audio processing is another advanced audio technique in Pygame, which involves applying digital signal processing (DSP) effects, filters, and transformations to sound effects and background music in real time to create unique audio effects, modify audio properties, or enhance the overall audio experience. Pygame provides support for real-time audio processing using the pygame.mixer.Sound class constructor and the pygame.mixer.Sound.play() function, allowing developers to apply DSP effects such as reverb, chorus, and equalization to sound effects and background music.

Additionally, Pygame provides support for integrating external audio libraries, plugins, and APIs into game projects to access advanced audio features, algorithms, and tools not available natively in Pygame. Developers can use external libraries such as FMOD, Wwise, or Pure Data (Pd) to implement advanced audio techniques such as procedural audio generation, real-time audio processing, and interactive music systems in their games, expanding the creative possibilities and capabilities of audio in Pygame.

Overall, advanced audio techniques in Pygame offer developers a wide range of tools, features, and strategies for creating immersive, interactive, and dynamic audio experiences in games. By understanding how to leverage spatial audio, dynamic mixing, procedural audio generation, real-time audio processing, and external audio libraries effectively, developers can create games with rich, engaging, and memorable audio landscapes that captivate players and enhance the overall gaming experience.

Chapter 6: Game Physics

6.1 Basics of Game Physics

UNDERSTANDING THE BASICS of game physics is crucial for creating realistic and engaging gameplay experiences in Pygame. Game physics governs the behavior of objects in the game world, including their movement, collisions, and interactions. In Pygame, developers can implement basic physics principles to simulate realistic motion, gravity, collisions, and other physical phenomena in their games.

One fundamental concept in game physics is the concept of motion, which describes how objects move and change position over time. In Pygame, developers can simulate motion by updating the position of game objects in the game loop based on their velocity and acceleration. By applying basic principles of kinematics, such as Newton's laws of motion, developers can create smooth and realistic motion effects for objects such as characters, projectiles, and obstacles in their games.

Gravity is another essential concept in game physics, which describes the force that attracts objects toward the center of the Earth or another massive body. In Pygame, developers can simulate gravity by applying a constant acceleration downward to objects in the game world. By incorporating gravity into the physics simulation, developers can create realistic jumping, falling, and projectile motion effects for characters and objects in their games, adding depth and immersion to the gameplay experience.

Collision detection and response are fundamental aspects of game physics, which involve detecting when two or more objects intersect and responding appropriately to the collision. In Pygame, developers can implement collision detection algorithms, such as bounding box collisions or pixel-perfect collisions, to detect when objects collide in the game world. Once a collision is detected, developers can implement collision response algorithms to handle the interaction between objects, such as bouncing off walls, destroying objects, or triggering game events.

In addition to basic physics principles, developers can also implement advanced physics effects in Pygame, such as elasticity, friction, and air resistance, to create more realistic and dynamic gameplay experiences. Elasticity describes the ability of objects to deform and bounce off each other when they collide, while friction describes the resistance to motion between surfaces in contact. By incorporating these effects into the physics simulation, developers can create more realistic and challenging gameplay scenarios, such as sliding on icy surfaces or bouncing off walls with different materials.

Another advanced physics concept in Pygame is the simulation of fluid dynamics, which involves simulating the behavior of liquids and gases in the game world. While Pygame does not provide built-in support for fluid dynamics, developers can implement custom physics algorithms and simulations to simulate fluid behavior, such as water flow, buoyancy, and viscosity. By incorporating fluid dynamics into their games, developers can create realistic water effects, weather simulations, and other immersive environmental effects that enhance the overall gameplay experience.

Overall, understanding the basics of game physics is essential for creating engaging and immersive gameplay experiences in Pygame. By applying principles of motion, gravity, collision detection, and advanced physics effects, developers can create games with realistic and dynamic physics simulations that captivate players and enhance the overall gaming experience.

6.2 Implementing Movement and Gravity

IMPLEMENTING MOVEMENT and gravity is crucial for creating dynamic and responsive gameplay in Pygame. Movement allows objects to traverse the game world, while gravity adds realism by pulling objects downward. In this section, we'll explore how to implement movement and gravity in Pygame to create engaging game experiences.

To implement movement in Pygame, developers typically update the position of game objects based on user input or predefined behaviors. For example, to move a character horizontally, you can modify its x-coordinate in the game loop according to keyboard input. Similarly, for vertical movement, you can adjust the y-coordinate based on user input or predefined behavior such as jumping.

```python
# Example of horizontal movement

if event.type == pygame.KEYDOWN:

if event.key == pygame.K_LEFT:

player_x -= player_speed

elif event.key == pygame.K_RIGHT:

player_x += player_speed
```

Gravity is implemented by applying a constant downward acceleration to objects in the game world. This acceleration affects the vertical motion of objects, causing them to fall toward the ground. To simulate gravity in Pygame, you can update the y-velocity of objects in the game loop to gradually increase their downward speed.

```python
# Example of applying gravity

if not on_ground:

player_y_velocity += gravity

player_y += player_y_velocity
```

In addition to basic movement and gravity, developers can enhance the player experience by incorporating more complex movement mechanics such as jumping, sliding, and dashing. These mechanics add depth and variety to gameplay, allowing players to navigate the game world in creative ways.

```python
# Example of jumping mechanics

if event.type == pygame.KEYDOWN:

if event.key == pygame.K_SPACE and on_ground:

player_y_velocity = -jump_strength
```

To prevent objects from moving through walls or other obstacles, collision detection is essential. By detecting collisions between objects and the environment, developers can ensure that movement is constrained by the game's geometry, adding realism and challenge to gameplay.

```python
# Example of collision detection

for wall in walls:

if player_rect.colliderect(wall):

# Handle collision

pass
```

Overall, implementing movement and gravity in Pygame is essential for creating immersive and dynamic gameplay experiences. By updating object positions, applying gravity, and incorporating collision detection, developers can create games that feel responsive, realistic, and engaging to players.

6.3 Handling Collisions and Overlaps

HANDLING COLLISIONS and overlaps is a critical aspect of game development, especially in Pygame, where accurate collision detection can make or break gameplay experiences. In this section, we'll explore various techniques and strategies for detecting and handling collisions between game objects in Pygame.

One common approach to collision detection in Pygame is bounding box collision detection, where collision is detected based on the rectangular bounding boxes surrounding game objects. This approach is simple and efficient but may not always provide accurate collision detection, especially for irregularly shaped objects.

 # Example of bounding box collision detection

if object1.rect.colliderect(object2.rect):

 # Handle collision

pass

For more precise collision detection, developers can use pixel-perfect collision detection, which involves checking for collisions at the pixel level. Pygame provides functions like pygame.sprite.collide_mask() to perform pixel-perfect collision detection between sprite objects, ensuring accurate collision detection even for objects with irregular shapes.

 # Example of pixel-perfect collision detection

if pygame.sprite.collide_mask(object1, object2):

 # Handle collision

pass

In addition to collision detection, developers must also handle collisions appropriately by responding to collisions in a way that makes sense for the game. This may involve applying physics-based responses such as bouncing off walls or platforms, destroying objects upon collision, or triggering game events.

```python
# Example of collision response

if pygame.sprite.collide_mask(player, enemy):

player.health -= enemy.damage

enemy.health -= player.damage
```

To optimize collision detection and improve performance, developers can implement spatial partitioning techniques such as quad trees or spatial hashing. These techniques reduce the number of collision checks by organizing game objects into spatial data structures, allowing for efficient culling of objects that are far apart or unlikely to collide.

```python
# Example of quad tree collision detection

quad_tree = QuadTree(0, pygame.Rect(0, 0, SCREEN_WIDTH, SCREEN_HEIGHT))

for object in objects:

quad_tree.insert(object)

# Check for collisions within a certain area

collidable_objects = quad_tree.retrieve(player.rect)

for object in collidable_objects:
```

```
if player.rect.colliderect(object.rect):
```

 # Handle collision

```
pass
```

In multiplayer games or games with complex physics interactions, developers may need to synchronize collisions between clients or simulate physics interactions on the server to ensure consistency across all game instances.

 # Example of server-side collision detection

```
if is_server:
```

```
for object1 in objects:
```

```
for object2 in objects:
```

```
if object1 != object2 and object1.rect.colliderect(object2.rect):
```

 # Handle collision

```
pass
```

Overall, handling collisions and overlaps effectively is essential for creating polished and enjoyable games in Pygame. By using appropriate collision detection techniques, responding to collisions appropriately, and optimizing collision detection for performance, developers can create games with immersive and responsive gameplay experiences.

6.4 Advanced Physics: Elasticity and Friction

ADVANCED PHYSICS CONCEPTS like elasticity and friction play crucial roles in creating realistic and immersive gameplay experiences in Pygame. In this section, we'll delve into how developers can implement these concepts to enhance the realism and complexity of their games.

Elasticity, also known as bounce or restitution, determines how objects behave when they collide with each other. In Pygame, developers can control the elasticity of objects by adjusting their coefficients of restitution. A coefficient of restitution of 1 represents perfect elasticity, where objects bounce off each other with no loss of energy, while a coefficient of restitution of 0 represents perfect inelasticity, where objects stick together upon collision.

 # Example of adjusting elasticity

object1.elasticity = 0.8

object2.elasticity = 0.5

Friction, on the other hand, represents the resistance to motion between surfaces in contact. In Pygame, developers can simulate friction by applying frictional forces to objects based on their surface properties and the coefficient of friction. Higher coefficients of friction result in greater resistance to motion, while lower coefficients allow objects to slide more easily.

 # Example of applying friction

object1.friction = 0.2

object2.friction = 0.5

By incorporating elasticity and friction into the physics simulation, developers can create more realistic and dynamic interactions between objects in their games. For example, objects with high elasticity will bounce off surfaces with more energy, leading to lively and exciting gameplay moments such as bouncing balls or collisions between vehicles.

 # Example of handling collisions with elasticity

if object1.rect.colliderect(object2.rect):

object1.velocity *= object1.elasticity

object2.velocity *= object2.elasticity

Similarly, friction affects how objects move across surfaces in the game world. Objects with higher friction coefficients will experience greater resistance to motion, causing them to slow down more quickly and slide less easily across surfaces.

 # Example of applying friction to movement

if on_ground:

object.velocity.x *= object.friction

In addition to elasticity and friction, developers can also simulate other advanced physics effects such as air resistance, buoyancy, and rotational dynamics to create even more realistic and immersive gameplay experiences. These effects add depth and complexity to the physics simulation, allowing for a wider range of gameplay mechanics and interactions.

 # Example of simulating air resistance

if not on_ground:

```
object.velocity.y -= air_resistance * object.velocity.y
```

Overall, by incorporating advanced physics concepts like elasticity and friction into their games, developers can create more realistic and engaging gameplay experiences in Pygame. By fine-tuning these parameters and simulating complex interactions between objects, developers can craft immersive worlds where players can truly feel the impact of their actions.

6.5 Creating Realistic Motion and Effects

CREATING REALISTIC motion and effects is essential for immersing players in the game world and enhancing the overall gaming experience in Pygame. In this section, we'll explore various techniques and strategies for implementing realistic motion and effects to make games more engaging and visually appealing.

One fundamental aspect of realistic motion is implementing smooth and natural animations for game objects. In Pygame, developers can achieve this by interpolating between different animation frames to create fluid motion. By updating the display at regular intervals and transitioning smoothly between frames, developers can create lifelike animations that enhance the realism of the game.

```python
# Example of interpolating animation frames

current_frame = 0

frame_duration = 100 # milliseconds

last_frame_change = pygame.time.get_ticks()

def animate():

global current_frame, last_frame_change

current_time = pygame.time.get_ticks()

if current_time - last_frame_change >= frame_duration:

current_frame = (current_frame + 1) % len(animation_frames)

last_frame_change = current_time

# Draw current_frame
```

screen.blit(animation_frames[current_frame], object_position)

Another important aspect of realistic motion is simulating inertia and momentum for moving objects. By applying acceleration and deceleration to objects based on player input or predefined behaviors, developers can create a sense of weight and responsiveness that mimics real-world physics.

 # Example of simulating inertia and momentum

if moving_forward:

object_velocity += acceleration * time_delta

else:

object_velocity -= deceleration * time_delta

object_position += object_velocity * time_delta

To further enhance the realism of motion, developers can incorporate visual effects such as particle systems, motion blur, and dynamic lighting. Particle systems allow developers to simulate phenomena like fire, smoke, and explosions, adding visual flair and dynamism to the game world.

 # Example of implementing a particle system

for particle **in** particles:

particle.update()

particle.draw(screen)

Motion blur can be achieved by rendering multiple frames of animation and blending them together to create a sense of motion blur. This technique is particularly effective for fast-moving objects such as vehicles or projectiles, where motion blur helps convey speed and momentum.

 # Example of implementing motion blur

blurred_frame = render_blurred_frame(current_frame, previous_frame, blur_amount)

screen.blit(blurred_frame, object_position)

Dynamic lighting effects can add depth and atmosphere to the game world by simulating light sources and casting realistic shadows. By adjusting the intensity and color of light sources dynamically, developers can create immersive environments that respond realistically to player actions and environmental conditions.

 # Example of implementing dynamic lighting

light_position = (x, y)

light_color = (255, 255, 255)

light_intensity = 0.8

light_radius = 100

pygame.draw.circle(screen, light_color, light_position, light_radius)

Overall, creating realistic motion and effects is crucial for immersing players in the game world and enhancing the overall gaming experience in Pygame. By implementing smooth animations, simulating inertia and momentum, and incorporating visual effects like particle systems and dynamic lighting, developers can create immersive and visually stunning games that captivate players' imaginations.

Chapter 7: Tile-based Games

7.1 Introduction to Tile-based Design

TILE-BASED GAME DESIGN is a popular approach used in many 2D games, including platformers, RPGs, and puzzle games. In this section, we'll explore the fundamentals of tile-based design and how it's implemented in Pygame.

At its core, tile-based design involves dividing the game world into a grid of equally sized tiles, where each tile represents a specific element or object in the game. These tiles can include terrain features such as ground, walls, and obstacles, as well as interactive elements like items, enemies, and NPCs.

In Pygame, tile-based games typically start with creating or loading a tile map, which is a grid-based representation of the game world composed of tiles. Tile maps can be created using specialized level editors or generated procedurally based on predefined rules and algorithms.

Example of loading a tile map

tile_map = load_tile_map("level1.tmx")

Once the tile map is loaded, developers can render it onto the game screen by iterating over the tiles in the map and drawing them at their respective positions. This process often involves using nested loops to traverse the rows and columns of the tile map and blitting the corresponding tile images onto the screen surface.

Example of rendering a tile map

for row in range(tile_map.height):

for col in range(tile_map.width):

```
tile = tile_map.get_tile(row, col)
```

```
screen.blit(tile.image, (col * TILE_SIZE, row * TILE_SIZE))
```

One of the main advantages of tile-based design is its simplicity and versatility. By using a grid-based approach, developers can easily create complex game worlds with intricate layouts and environments. Additionally, tile-based design allows for efficient memory usage and rendering, as only the visible tiles need to be loaded and drawn at any given time.

Tile-based design also facilitates level design and iteration, as developers can quickly prototype and modify game levels by rearranging tiles or adjusting their properties. This flexibility allows for rapid iteration and experimentation during the game development process, leading to more polished and refined game experiences.

In addition to static tiles, tile-based design often involves using tilesets, which are collections of reusable tiles that represent various game elements and objects. Tilesets allow developers to create diverse and visually appealing game worlds by mixing and matching tiles to create unique environments and landscapes.

 # Example of using tilesets

```
ground_tile = tileset.get_tile("ground")
```

```
wall_tile = tileset.get_tile("wall")
```

```
player_tile = tileset.get_tile("player")
```

Another key aspect of tile-based design is collision detection and handling. Since the game world is divided into a grid of tiles, collision detection can be simplified by checking for collisions between the player or other game objects and the tiles themselves.

This approach allows for efficient and accurate collision detection, particularly in games with simple geometric shapes.

 # Example of tile-based collision detection

player_rect = player.get_rect()

for row **in** range(tile_map.height):

for col **in** range(tile_map.width):

if tile_map.get_tile(row, col).collides_with(player_rect):

 # Handle collision

pass

Overall, tile-based design is a versatile and effective approach for creating 2D games in Pygame. By dividing the game world into a grid of tiles and leveraging tile maps, tilesets, and efficient collision detection, developers can create immersive and visually stunning game experiences that captivate players' imaginations.

7.2 Creating a Tile Map

CREATING A TILE MAP is a fundamental step in developing tile-based games in Pygame. In this section, we'll explore the process of creating a tile map, which serves as the foundation for constructing the game world.

Tile maps are typically created using specialized level editors or generated procedurally based on predefined rules and algorithms. The tile map consists of a grid of tiles, where each tile represents a specific element or object in the game world, such as terrain features, obstacles, items, or interactive elements.

In Pygame, tile maps are often represented using data structures such as arrays, lists, or dictionaries, where each element corresponds to a tile at a specific position in the grid. These data structures allow developers to efficiently store and manipulate the tile map data, making it easy to render and interact with the game world.

```python
# Example of creating a tile map using a 2D array

tile_map = [

[1, 1, 1, 1, 1],

[1, 0, 0, 0, 1],

[1, 0, 1, 0, 1],

[1, 0, 0, 0, 1],

[1, 1, 1, 1, 1]

]
```

Each number or value in the tile map data represents a different tile type or tile ID, which corresponds to a specific tile image or tileset. By defining a mapping between tile IDs and tile images, developers can easily render the tile map onto the game screen.

```
# Example of rendering a tile map using a tileset

tileset = load_tileset("tileset.png", tile_width, tile_height)

for row in range(len(tile_map)):

for col in range(len(tile_map[row])):

tile_id = tile_map[row][col]

tile_image = tileset.get_tile_image(tile_id)

screen.blit(tile_image, (col * tile_width, row * tile_height))
```

In addition to static tiles, tile maps often include layers for different types of game elements, such as terrain, background, objects, and decorations. By using multiple layers, developers can create visually rich and immersive game worlds with depth and complexity.

```
# Example of creating multiple layers in a tile map

terrain_layer = [

[1, 1, 1, 1, 1],

[1, 0, 0, 0, 1],

[1, 0, 1, 0, 1],

[1, 0, 0, 0, 1],

[1, 1, 1, 1, 1]
```

```
]

object_layer = [

[0, 0, 0, 0, 0],

[0, 2, 0, 0, 0],

[0, 0, 0, 3, 0],

[0, 0, 0, 0, 0],

[0, 0, 0, 0, 0]

]
```

Each layer can be rendered separately onto the game screen, allowing developers to control the order and visibility of different elements in the game world. This layer-based approach provides flexibility and versatility in designing and composing game levels.

 # Example of rendering multiple layers in a tile map

```
render_layer(terrain_layer)

render_layer(object_layer)
```

Overall, creating a tile map is a crucial step in developing tile-based games in Pygame. By defining the layout and composition of the game world using a grid-based tile map, developers can construct immersive and visually engaging game environments that captivate players' imaginations.

7.3 Implementing Tile-based Collision Detection

TILE-BASED COLLISION detection is a fundamental aspect of tile-based games in Pygame. In this section, we'll explore how to implement collision detection between game objects and the tiles in the tile map.

The basic idea behind tile-based collision detection is to check whether a game object's bounding box intersects with any solid tiles in the tile map. Solid tiles typically represent impassable terrain or obstacles that game objects cannot move through.

```python
# Example of tile-based collision detection

player_rect = player.get_rect()

for row in range(len(tile_map)):

for col in range(len(tile_map[row])):

if tile_map[row][col] == SOLID_TILE_ID:

tile_rect = Rect(col * TILE_SIZE, row * TILE_SIZE, TILE_SIZE, TILE_SIZE)

if player_rect.colliderect(tile_rect):

# Collision detected, handle accordingly

pass
```

One common approach to tile-based collision detection is to iterate over the tiles in the tile map and check whether the player's bounding box intersects with the bounding box of any solid tiles. If a collision is detected, the game can then respond accordingly, such as preventing the player from moving into the solid tile or triggering a collision event.

 # Example of handling tile-based collisions

for row **in** range(len(tile_map)):

for col **in** range(len(tile_map[row])):

if tile_map[row][col] == SOLID_TILE_ID:

tile_rect = Rect(col * TILE_SIZE, row * TILE_SIZE, TILE_SIZE, TILE_SIZE)

if player_rect.colliderect(tile_rect):

 # Player collided with a solid tile, handle accordingly

player.handle_collision()

In addition to simple bounding box collisions, tile-based collision detection can also involve more complex collision shapes and behaviors, such as sloped tiles, one-way platforms, or tiles with varying heights or depths. Implementing these features often requires additional logic and calculations to accurately detect and resolve collisions between game objects and tiles.

 # Example of handling complex tile-based collisions

for row **in** range(len(tile_map)):

for col **in** range(len(tile_map[row])):

tile_type = tile_map[row][col]

if tile_type == SLOPED_TILE_ID:

 # Check for collision with sloped tile and adjust player's position and velocity

pass

elif tile_type == ONE_WAY_PLATFORM_ID:

 # Check for collision with one-way platform and allow player to pass through from below

pass

Overall, tile-based collision detection is a powerful technique for creating realistic and immersive game worlds in Pygame. By checking for collisions between game objects and the tiles in the tile map, developers can create challenging and engaging gameplay experiences that keep players coming back for more.

7.4 Designing Levels with Tiles

DESIGNING LEVELS WITH tiles is a crucial aspect of developing tile-based games in Pygame. In this section, we'll explore various strategies and techniques for designing compelling and engaging game levels using tiles.

One common approach to level design with tiles is to create reusable tilesets containing a variety of tiles representing different terrain features, objects, decorations, and interactive elements. By designing tiles that seamlessly fit together and align with the grid-based layout of the game world, developers can easily assemble and customize game levels using a combination of tiles.

 # Example of designing a level using tiles

```
level_data = [

[1, 1, 1, 1, 1],

[1, 0, 0, 0, 1],

[1, 0, 1, 0, 1],

[1, 0, 0, 0, 1],

[1, 1, 1, 1, 1]

]
```

In addition to basic terrain tiles, level designers can also incorporate a variety of interactive elements and obstacles, such as platforms, spikes, switches, doors, keys, and enemies. By carefully placing these elements within the level and designing challenges and puzzles

around them, developers can create dynamic and engaging gameplay
experiences that test players' skills and reflexes.

 # Example of designing a level with interactive elements

level_data = [

[1, 1, 1, 1, 1],

[1, 0, 0, 0, 1],

[1, 0, 2, 0, 1],

[1, 0, 3, 0, 1],

[1, 1, 1, 1, 1]

]

Another important aspect of level design with tiles is the concept
of pacing and progression. By carefully structuring the layout of
the level and controlling the distribution and arrangement of tiles,
developers can create a sense of flow and rhythm that guides players
through the game experience, introducing new challenges and
obstacles at strategic intervals to maintain engagement and
excitement.

 # Example of designing a level with pacing and progression

level_data = [

[1, 1, 1, 1, 1],

[1, 0, 0, 0, 1],

[1, 0, 2, 0, 1],

[1, 0, 0, 3, 1],

```
[1, 1, 1, 1, 1]

]
```

Furthermore, level designers can leverage principles of visual storytelling and environmental storytelling to convey narrative and thematic elements through the design of the game world. By using tiles to create immersive and atmospheric environments, developers can enhance the player experience and evoke emotions and reactions that deepen their connection to the game world and its characters.

```
# Example of designing a level with visual storytelling
level_data = [

[1, 1, 1, 1, 1],

[1, 0, 0, 0, 1],

[1, 0, 4, 0, 1],

[1, 0, 0, 0, 1],

[1, 1, 1, 1, 1]

]
```

Overall, designing levels with tiles is a creative and iterative process that requires careful consideration of gameplay mechanics, aesthetics, and player experience. By embracing the flexibility and versatility of tile-based level design, developers can craft memorable and immersive game worlds that captivate players' imaginations and keep them coming back for more.

7.5 Advanced Tile Techniques: Parallax Scrolling and Layering

PARALLAX SCROLLING and layering are advanced techniques used in tile-based game development to create depth and visual interest in the game environment. In this section, we'll explore how these techniques work and how to implement them effectively in Pygame.

Parallax scrolling is a visual effect where background layers move at different speeds to create an illusion of depth. This effect is commonly used to simulate the perception of distance and motion in 2D games. By moving background layers slower than foreground layers, developers can create a sense of depth and immersion that enhances the overall visual experience of the game.

```python
# Example of parallax scrolling implementation

foreground_scroll_speed = 5

background_scroll_speed = 2

def update_background():

background_x -= background_scroll_speed

if background_x <= -background_width:

background_x = 0

def update_foreground():

foreground_x -= foreground_scroll_speed

if foreground_x <= -foreground_width:
```

```
foreground_x = 0
```

Layering, on the other hand, involves organizing tiles into distinct layers that are rendered in a specific order to create depth and perspective in the game world. By separating tiles into different layers based on their position relative to the player, developers can control how objects interact with each other and create visual effects such as overlapping and occlusion.

```
# Example of layering implementation

background_layer = pygame.sprite.LayeredUpdates()

foreground_layer = pygame.sprite.LayeredUpdates()

# Add tiles to respective layers

for tile in level.tiles:

if tile.layer == 'background':

background_layer.add(tile)

elif tile.layer == 'foreground':

foreground_layer.add(tile)

# Render layers in order

background_layer.draw(screen)

player.draw(screen)

foreground_layer.draw(screen)
```

By combining parallax scrolling and layering techniques, developers can create visually stunning and immersive game environments that capture the player's attention and enhance their gaming experience.

Whether it's a sprawling landscape, a bustling cityscape, or a mystical dungeon, these techniques allow developers to bring their game worlds to life with depth, detail, and dynamism.

 # Example of combining parallax scrolling and layering

update_background()

background_layer.draw(screen)

update_foreground()

foreground_layer.draw(screen)

player.draw(screen)

In conclusion, parallax scrolling and layering are powerful tools in the arsenal of tile-based game developers. By mastering these techniques and using them creatively, developers can elevate the visual quality and immersive appeal of their games, creating memorable and captivating experiences for players to enjoy.

Chapter 8: User Interfaces and Menus

8.1 Designing a Game Menu

DESIGNING A GAME MENU is a crucial aspect of game development as it serves as the gateway for players to access various game features and settings. A well-designed menu not only provides functionality but also enhances the overall user experience by being intuitive, visually appealing, and easy to navigate.

```python
# Example of a simple game menu layout

menu_options = ["Start Game", "Options", "Exit"]

def draw_menu():

menu_surface.fill((0, 0, 0))  # Fill menu surface with black

for i, option in enumerate(menu_options):

text_surface = font.render(option, True, (255, 255, 255))

text_rect = text_surface.get_rect(center=(menu_width / 2, menu_height / 2 + i * 40))

menu_surface.blit(text_surface, text_rect)
```

One of the key considerations when designing a game menu is the layout and organization of menu elements. It's essential to structure the menu in a logical and intuitive manner, grouping related options together and providing clear navigation paths for users to follow. Additionally, using visual cues such as icons, buttons, and separators can help differentiate menu sections and guide user interaction.

```python
# Example of adding icons to menu options

menu_options = [("Start Game", start_icon), ("Options", options_icon), ("Exit", exit_icon)]
```

```python
def draw_menu():

menu_surface.fill((0, 0, 0)) # Fill menu surface with black

for i, (option, icon) in enumerate(menu_options):

text_surface = font.render(option, True, (255, 255, 255))

text_rect = text_surface.get_rect(center=(menu_width / 2,
menu_height / 2 + i * 40))

menu_surface.blit(text_surface, text_rect)

menu_surface.blit(icon, (text_rect.left - icon.get_width() - 10,
text_rect.centery - icon.get_height() / 2))
```

Another important aspect of menu design is visual aesthetics. Using appropriate colors, fonts, and graphical elements can significantly enhance the visual appeal of the menu and contribute to the overall theme and style of the game. Moreover, incorporating animations and transitions can add polish and flair to the menu, making it more engaging and memorable for players.

```python
# Example of adding transitions to menu elements

def draw_menu():

menu_surface.fill((0, 0, 0)) # Fill menu surface with black

for i, option in enumerate(menu_options):

text_surface = font.render(option, True, (255, 255, 255))

text_rect = text_surface.get_rect(center=(menu_width / 2,
menu_height / 2 + i * 40))

text_rect.y -= menu_offset # Apply vertical offset for animation
```

```python
menu_surface.blit(text_surface, text_rect)
```

Additionally, it's essential to consider the functionality and usability of the menu. Providing clear instructions, tooltips, and feedback can help users understand how to navigate the menu and make informed decisions. Moreover, ensuring that menu elements are responsive to user input and accessible across different devices and platforms can improve usability and accessibility for a broader audience.

```python
# Example of adding tooltips to menu options

menu_options = [("Start Game", start_icon, "Begin your adventure"), ("Options", options_icon, "Adjust game settings"), ("Exit", exit_icon, "Quit the game")]

def draw_menu():

menu_surface.fill((0, 0, 0)) # Fill menu surface with black

for i, (option, icon, tooltip) in enumerate(menu_options):

text_surface = font.render(option, True, (255, 255, 255))

text_rect = text_surface.get_rect(center=(menu_width / 2, menu_height / 2 + i * 40))

text_rect.y -= menu_offset # Apply vertical offset for animation

menu_surface.blit(text_surface, text_rect)

if text_rect.collidepoint(mouse_pos):

tooltip_surface = font_small.render(tooltip, True, (255, 255, 255))

tooltip_rect = tooltip_surface.get_rect(midtop=(menu_width / 2, text_rect.bottom + 5))

menu_surface.blit(tooltip_surface, tooltip_rect)
```

In conclusion, designing a game menu requires careful consideration of layout, aesthetics, functionality, and usability. By following principles of user-centered design and incorporating feedback from playtesting and user testing, developers can create menus that not only serve as effective navigational tools but also enhance the overall player experience and immersion in the game.

8.2 Creating Buttons and Interactive Elements

CREATING BUTTONS AND interactive elements in a game menu is essential for providing users with intuitive controls and feedback. Buttons serve as actionable items that users can click or tap to perform specific actions, such as starting the game, accessing options, or exiting the application. In this section, we'll explore how to design and implement interactive elements using Pygame.

Buttons can be implemented using simple rectangular shapes or custom graphical assets, such as images or sprites. When designing buttons, it's crucial to consider their size, shape, color, and placement to ensure they are visually distinct and easily recognizable to users. Additionally, providing visual feedback, such as highlighting or changing the appearance of buttons when hovered over or clicked, can improve usability and interactivity.

 # Example of creating a basic rectangular button

class Button:

def __init__(self, text, position, size, color, highlight_color, font, action):

self.text = text

self.position = position

self.size = size

self.color = color

self.highlight_color = highlight_color

```python
        self.font = font

        self.action = action

    def draw(self, surface, mouse_pos):

        rect = pygame.Rect(self.position, self.size)

        if rect.collidepoint(mouse_pos):

            pygame.draw.rect(surface, self.highlight_color, rect)

        else:

            pygame.draw.rect(surface, self.color, rect)

        text_surface = self.font.render(self.text, True, (255, 255, 255))

        text_rect = text_surface.get_rect(center=rect.center)

        surface.blit(text_surface, text_rect)

    def handle_event(self, event):

        if event.type == pygame.MOUSEBUTTONDOWN:

            if self.position[0] < event.pos[0] < self.position[0] + self.size[0] and \

               self.position[1] < event.pos[1] < self.position[1] + self.size[1]:

                self.action()
```

Interactive elements can also include sliders, checkboxes, dropdown menus, and other input controls commonly found in user interfaces. These elements allow users to adjust settings, toggle options, and customize their gameplay experience. Implementing these elements requires handling user input and updating game state accordingly.

```python
# Example of implementing a slider control

class Slider:

def __init__(self, position, width, height, min_value, max_value, initial_value, color):

self.position = position

self.width = width

self.height = height

self.min_value = min_value

self.max_value = max_value

self.value = initial_value

self.color = color

def draw(self, surface):

pygame.draw.rect(surface, (100, 100, 100), (self.position[0], self.position[1], self.width, self.height))

pygame.draw.rect(surface, self.color, (self.position[0], self.position[1],

int((self.value - self.min_value) / (self.max_value - self.min_value) * self.width), self.height))

def handle_event(self, event):

if event.type == pygame.MOUSEBUTTONDOWN:

if self.position[0] < event.pos[0] < self.position[0] + self.width and \
```

self.position[1] < event.pos[1] < self.position[1] + self.height:

self.value = min(self.max_value, max(self.min_value, (event.pos[0] - self.position[0]) / self.width * (self.max_value - self.min_value) + self.min_value))

In summary, creating buttons and interactive elements in a game menu involves designing visually appealing and intuitive controls that respond to user input. By carefully considering the design and implementation of these elements, developers can enhance the usability and interactivity of their games, providing players with a more engaging and enjoyable experience.

8.3 Implementing a Scoring System

IMPLEMENTING A SCORING system is crucial for many games as it provides players with feedback on their performance and encourages replayability by allowing them to compete for higher scores. In this section, we'll discuss how to design and implement a scoring system in a Pygame-based game.

A scoring system typically involves tracking various in-game actions or achievements and assigning points to them. These actions could include collecting items, defeating enemies, completing objectives, or achieving specific milestones within the game. Points are awarded based on the difficulty or significance of the action, with more challenging tasks typically yielding higher scores.

 # Example of a simple scoring system

```python
class ScoringSystem:

def __init__(self):

self.score = 0

def add_points(self, points):

self.score += points

def reset_score(self):

self.score = 0
```

The scoring system should be integrated into the game's logic to update the player's score dynamically as they progress through the game. This involves calling the appropriate methods of the scoring system class whenever relevant events occur in the game.

```python
# Example of updating the score in response to game events

class Game:

def __init__(self):

self.scoring_system = ScoringSystem()

def player_collects_item(self):

# Increment the score when the player collects an item

self.scoring_system.add_points(10)

def player_defeats_enemy(self):

# Increase the score when the player defeats an enemy

self.scoring_system.add_points(50)

def display_score(self):

# Display the current score on the screen

score_text = f"Score: {self.scoring_system.score}"

# Code to render and display the score text on the game screen
```

Additionally, the scoring system should be integrated with the game's user interface to provide real-time feedback to the player. This usually involves displaying the current score prominently on the game screen, updating it as the player earns points.

Scoring systems can also include features such as multipliers, combo bonuses, or penalties for mistakes to add depth and complexity to the scoring mechanics. These elements can enhance gameplay by rewarding skillful play and encouraging strategic decision-making.

```python
# Example of implementing a combo system in the scoring system

class ScoringSystem:

    def __init__(self):

        self.score = 0

        self.combo = 0

    def add_points(self, points):

        self.score += points * (self.combo + 1)

        self.combo += 1

    def reset_combo(self):

        self.combo = 0

    def reset_score(self):

        self.score = 0
```

In summary, implementing a scoring system involves designing a mechanism for assigning points to in-game actions and integrating it into the game's logic and user interface. By providing players with a clear and meaningful way to track their progress and achievements, a scoring system can enhance the overall experience and engagement of the game.

Designing a Game Menu

IN THIS SECTION, WE will delve into the process of designing a game menu, an essential component of any game that provides players with options to start, pause, resume, and exit the game, as well as access additional features such as settings and help.

A well-designed game menu serves as the gateway to the game, providing players with a visually appealing and intuitive interface to navigate the various options and functionalities available to them.

```python
# Example of a simple game menu design

class GameMenu:

def __init__(self):

self.options = ["Start Game", "Settings", "Help", "Exit Game"]

def display_menu(self):

print("Main Menu:")

for i, option in enumerate(self.options):

print(f"{i + 1}. {option}")

def handle_input(self, choice):

if choice == 1:

# Start the game

print("Starting the game...")

elif choice == 2:
```

```python
# Display settings
print("Displaying settings...")
elif choice == 3:
# Display help
print("Displaying help...")
elif choice == 4:
# Exit the game
print("Exiting the game...")
else:
print("Invalid choice. Please select a valid option.")
```

The game menu should be visually appealing and consistent with the game's theme and aesthetics. This involves choosing appropriate fonts, colors, and graphical elements to create a cohesive visual design that enhances the overall player experience.

```python
# Example of incorporating visual design into the game menu
class GameMenu:
def __init__(self):
self.options = ["Start Game", "Settings", "Help", "Exit Game"]
self.font = pygame.font.Font("arial.ttf", 24)
self.selected_option = 0
def display_menu(self):
```

```python
for i, option in enumerate(self.options):

    text = self.font.render(option, True, (255, 255, 255))

    if i == self.selected_option:

        # Highlight the selected option

        text = self.font.render(option, True, (255, 0, 0))

    # Code to render and display the text on the menu screen

def handle_input(self, event):

    if event.type == pygame.KEYDOWN:

        if event.key == pygame.K_UP:

            self.selected_option = (self.selected_option - 1) % len(self.options)

        elif event.key == pygame.K_DOWN:

            self.selected_option = (self.selected_option + 1) % len(self.options)

        elif event.key == pygame.K_RETURN:

            # Execute the selected option

            if self.selected_option == 0:

                print("Starting the game...")

            elif self.selected_option == 1:

                print("Displaying settings...")

            elif self.selected_option == 2:

                print("Displaying help...")
```

```python
elif self.selected_option == 3:

print("Exiting the game...")
```

Furthermore, the game menu should be responsive to player input, allowing them to navigate the menu options using keyboard, mouse, or touchscreen controls. This involves implementing event handling logic to detect and respond to user actions such as button presses or mouse clicks.

```python
# Example of handling user input in the game menu

class GameMenu:

def __init__(self):

self.options = ["Start Game", "Settings", "Help", "Exit Game"]

self.selected_option = 0

def handle_input(self, event):

if event.type == pygame.KEYDOWN:

if event.key == pygame.K_UP:

self.selected_option = (self.selected_option - 1) % len(self.options)

elif event.key == pygame.K_DOWN:

self.selected_option = (self.selected_option + 1) % len(self.options)

elif event.key == pygame.K_RETURN:

# Execute the selected option

if self.selected_option == 0:

print("Starting the game...")
```

```python
elif self.selected_option == 1:

print("Displaying settings...")

elif self.selected_option == 2:

print("Displaying help...")

elif self.selected_option == 3:

print("Exiting the game...")
```

In summary, designing a game menu involves creating a visually appealing and intuitive interface for players to navigate the various options and functionalities available in the game. By carefully considering factors such as visual design, responsiveness to user input, and consistency with the game's theme, developers can create a menu that enhances the overall player experience and sets the tone for the rest of the game.

Advanced UI Techniques: Dialogs and Tooltips

IN THIS SECTION, WE will explore advanced user interface (UI) techniques involving dialogs and tooltips, which are essential components for providing additional information and interactions within a game.

Dialogs are modal windows that temporarily interrupt the main workflow to display critical information or prompt the player for input. They are commonly used for tasks such as confirming actions, displaying notifications, or presenting important messages to the player.

```python
# Example of a simple dialog implementation

class Dialog:

def __init__(self, message):

self.message = message

def display(self):

# Code to render and display the dialog window with the message

pass

# Example usage

confirmation_dialog = Dialog("Are you sure you want to quit?")

confirmation_dialog.display()
```

Tooltips are small, contextual overlays that provide additional information when the player hovers over or interacts with specific elements in the game. They are useful for explaining the functionality of buttons, icons, or other interactive elements and can enhance the player's understanding of the game mechanics.

```python
# Example of a tooltip implementation

class Tooltip:

def __init__(self, text, position):

self.text = text

self.position = position

def display(self):

# Code to render and display the tooltip at the specified position

pass

# Example usage

start_button_tooltip = Tooltip("Start the game", (100, 100))

start_button_tooltip.display()
```

Dialogs and tooltips should be designed to be unobtrusive and visually consistent with the overall game interface. This involves choosing appropriate colors, fonts, and graphical elements to ensure that they blend seamlessly with the rest of the UI.

```python
# Example of styling dialogs and tooltips

class Dialog:

def __init__(self, message):

self.message = message
```

```python
self.font = pygame.font.Font("arial.ttf", 16)

self.color = (255, 255, 255)

self.background_color = (0, 0, 0)

self.border_color = (255, 0, 0)

def display(self):

# Code to render and display the dialog window with styled text and background

pass

class Tooltip:

def __init__(self, text, position):

self.text = text

self.position = position

self.font = pygame.font.Font("arial.ttf", 12)

self.color = (255, 255, 255)

self.background_color = (0, 0, 0)

def display(self):

# Code to render and display the tooltip with styled text and background

pass
```

Additionally, dialogs and tooltips should be implemented in a way that ensures they do not obstruct important game elements or interfere with the player's interaction with the game. This may involve positioning them strategically on the screen and providing options for the player to dismiss or close them easily.

```python
# Example of positioning dialogs and tooltips on the screen

class Dialog:

def __init__(self, message, position):

self.message = message

self.position = position

def display(self):

# Code to render and display the dialog window at the specified position

pass

class Tooltip:

def __init__(self, text, position):

self.text = text

self.position = position

def display(self):

# Code to render and display the tooltip near the specified position

pass
```

In summary, dialogs and tooltips are powerful UI components that can enhance the player experience by providing additional information and interactions within the game. By carefully designing and implementing them with attention to detail, developers can create a more intuitive and immersive gameplay experience for players.

Chapter 9: State Management

Understanding Game States

IN GAME DEVELOPMENT, managing various states of the game is crucial for maintaining a structured and coherent gameplay experience. A game state represents a specific condition or situation within the game, such as the main menu, gameplay, pause menu, game over screen, etc. Each state typically has its own set of rules, interactions, and visuals, and transitioning between states smoothly is essential for seamless gameplay.

Managing game states involves identifying and defining the different states that the game can be in, implementing logic to handle state transitions, and updating the game components accordingly based on the current state. This approach helps organize the codebase, improves maintainability, and facilitates the addition of new features or content to the game.

```python
# Example of defining game states

class State:

def __init__(self, name):

self.name = name

class MenuState(State):

def __init__(self):

super().__init__("Menu")

class GameState(State):

def __init__(self):

super().__init__("Game")
```

```python
class PauseState(State):

def __init__(self):

super().__init__("Pause")

# Example usage

current_state = MenuState()
```

Implementing a state machine is a common technique for managing game states effectively. A state machine consists of a set of states and rules for transitioning between them based on certain conditions or events. This allows for a clear and structured flow of gameplay, where each state knows how to handle its specific tasks and when to transition to other states.

```python
# Example of a simple state machine

class StateMachine:

def __init__(self):

self.states = {}

self.current_state = None

def add_state(self, state):

self.states[state.name] = state

def set_state(self, state_name):

if state_name in self.states:

self.current_state = self.states[state_name]

else:
```

```python
print(f"Error: State '{state_name}' does not exist")

# Example usage

game_state_machine = StateMachine()

game_state_machine.add_state(MenuState())

game_state_machine.add_state(GameState())

game_state_machine.add_state(PauseState())

game_state_machine.set_state("Menu")
```

Transitions between states can be triggered by various events or conditions, such as user input, game events, or predefined triggers. By defining clear rules for state transitions and handling them appropriately in the code, developers can ensure that the game progresses smoothly and responds accurately to player actions.

```python
# Example of handling state transitions

class Game:

def __init__(self):

self.state_machine = StateMachine()

def handle_input(self, input_event):

if input_event == "start_game":

self.state_machine.set_state("Game")

elif input_event == "pause_game":

self.state_machine.set_state("Pause")

elif input_event == "resume_game":
```

```
self.state_machine.set_state("Game")
```

 # Example usage

```
game = Game()
```

```
game.handle_input("start_game")
```

In summary, state management is a fundamental aspect of game development that involves organizing and controlling the various states of the game to ensure a coherent and enjoyable gameplay experience. By implementing a state machine and handling state transitions effectively, developers can create engaging and immersive games with structured and intuitive gameplay flows.

Implementing a State Machine

IMPLEMENTING A STATE machine is a foundational aspect of managing game states in game development. A state machine consists of a set of states and rules for transitioning between them based on specific conditions or events. This approach provides a structured way to control the flow of the game and ensure that it responds appropriately to player interactions.

Creating a state machine involves defining the states of the game and the rules for transitioning between them. Each state typically encapsulates the behavior and logic relevant to that specific game state, such as the main menu, gameplay, pause menu, etc. The state machine itself manages the current state of the game and facilitates transitions between states.

```python
# Example of a simple state machine implementation in Python

class StateMachine:

    def __init__(self):

        self.states = {}

        self.current_state = None

    def add_state(self, state):

        self.states[state.name] = state

    def set_state(self, state_name):

        if state_name in self.states:

            self.current_state = self.states[state_name]
```

```python
else:
    print(f"Error: State '{state_name}' does not exist")

# Example usage
game_state_machine = StateMachine()
game_state_machine.add_state(MenuState())
game_state_machine.add_state(GameState())
game_state_machine.add_state(PauseState())
game_state_machine.set_state("Menu")
```

In the above example, we define a StateMachine class that maintains a dictionary of available states and the current state of the game. The add_state method allows us to add new states to the state machine, while the set_state method transitions the game to the specified state if it exists in the dictionary.

```python
# Example of defining game states
class State:
    def __init__(self, name):
        self.name = name

class MenuState(State):
    def __init__(self):
        super().__init__("Menu")

class GameState(State):
    def __init__(self):
```

```python
super().__init__("Game")

class PauseState(State):

def __init__(self):

super().__init__("Pause")
```

Each state is represented by a class that inherits from a base State class. This allows for encapsulation of state-specific behavior and attributes. For instance, the MenuState, GameState, and PauseState classes represent different states of the game, such as the main menu, gameplay, and pause menu, respectively.

```python
# Example usage

game_state_machine = StateMachine()

game_state_machine.add_state(MenuState())

game_state_machine.add_state(GameState())

game_state_machine.add_state(PauseState())

game_state_machine.set_state("Menu")
```

Finally, we create an instance of the StateMachine class and add the desired states to it. We then set the initial state of the game to the main menu using the set_state method. This sets up the initial state of the game and prepares it for further interactions and state transitions during gameplay.

Transitioning Between Game Scenes

TRANSITIONING BETWEEN game scenes is a crucial aspect of game development, allowing for seamless progression from one part of the game to another. Game scenes represent distinct sections of gameplay, such as levels, menus, cutscenes, etc. Properly managing scene transitions ensures a smooth player experience and enables developers to organize and structure their games effectively.

In most game engines and frameworks, scene management involves loading and unloading resources associated with each scene, updating the game state, and transitioning the player seamlessly between scenes. This process may also include transitioning animations, music, and other elements to maintain continuity and immersion.

```python
# Example of a scene manager implementation in Python

class SceneManager:

def __init__(self):

self.scenes = {}

self.current_scene = None

def add_scene(self, scene):

self.scenes[scene.name] = scene

def set_scene(self, scene_name):

if scene_name in self.scenes:

self.current_scene = self.scenes[scene_name]
```

```python
self.current_scene.load()

else:

print(f"Error: Scene '{scene_name}' does not exist")

# Example usage

scene_manager = SceneManager()

scene_manager.add_scene(MenuScene())

scene_manager.add_scene(Level1Scene())

scene_manager.add_scene(GameOverScene())

scene_manager.set_scene("Menu")
```

In the above example, we define a SceneManager class responsible for managing game scenes. It maintains a dictionary of available scenes and handles the transition between them. The add_scene method allows us to add new scenes to the scene manager, while the set_scene method transitions the game to the specified scene by loading its resources and updating the current scene.

```python
# Example of defining game scenes

class Scene:

def __init__(self, name):

self.name = name

def load(self):

pass

class MenuScene(Scene):
```

```python
def __init__(self):

super().__init__("Menu")

def load(self):

# Load menu resources

pass

class Level1Scene(Scene):

def __init__(self):

super().__init__("Level1")

def load(self):

# Load level 1 resources

pass

class GameOverScene(Scene):

def __init__(self):

super().__init__("GameOver")

def load(self):

# Load game over screen resources

pass
```

Each scene is represented by a class that inherits from a base Scene class. The load method of each scene class is responsible for loading the necessary resources when the scene is activated. This ensures that resources are loaded efficiently and only when needed, optimizing memory usage and performance.

```python
# Example usage

scene_manager = SceneManager()

scene_manager.add_scene(MenuScene())

scene_manager.add_scene(Level1Scene())

scene_manager.add_scene(GameOverScene())

scene_manager.set_scene("Menu")
```

Finally, we create an instance of the SceneManager class and add the desired scenes to it. We then set the initial scene of the game to the main menu using the set_scene method. This sets up the initial state of the game and prepares it for further interactions and scene transitions during gameplay.

Managing Game Sessions and Progress

MANAGING GAME SESSIONS and progress is essential for creating immersive gaming experiences and retaining player engagement. Game sessions refer to individual playthroughs of a game, while progress encompasses the player's advancement within the game, including achievements, unlocked content, and saved state.

Saving Game Progress

SAVING GAME PROGRESS allows players to continue their gaming experience from where they left off, even after exiting the game. This typically involves saving relevant game data, such as player statistics, inventory, level progression, and any other relevant information, to a persistent storage medium, such as a file or database.

```python
# Example of saving game progress to a file

import json

def save_game_progress(player_data, file_path):

with open(file_path, 'w') as file:

json.dump(player_data, file)

# Example usage

player_data = {

'level': 5,

'experience': 2500,
```

'inventory': ['sword', 'shield', 'potion']

}

save_game_progress(player_data, 'save_data.json')

In the above example, the save_game_progress function takes player data in the form of a dictionary and saves it to a JSON file. This file can later be loaded to restore the player's progress.

Loading Saved Game Data

LOADING SAVED GAME data restores the player's progress and allows them to continue playing from where they left off. This involves reading the saved data from the storage medium and updating the game state accordingly.

 # Example of loading saved game data from a file

def load_game_progress(file_path):

with open(file_path, 'r') **as** file:

return json.load(file)

 # Example usage

loaded_data = load_game_progress('save_data.json')

print(loaded_data)

The load_game_progress function reads the saved data from the JSON file and returns it as a dictionary, which can then be used to update the game state.

Managing Multiple Save Slots

OFFERING MULTIPLE SAVE slots allows players to create and manage multiple game sessions simultaneously, providing flexibility and convenience. Each save slot can store independent game progress, allowing players to explore different playthroughs or share the game with others without affecting their main progress.

```python
# Example of managing multiple save slots

def save_game_progress(player_data, slot_number, file_prefix):

    file_path = f"{file_prefix}_{slot_number}.json"

    with open(file_path, 'w') as file:

        json.dump(player_data, file)

def load_game_progress(slot_number, file_prefix):

    file_path = f"{file_prefix}_{slot_number}.json"

    with open(file_path, 'r') as file:

        return json.load(file)

# Example usage

save_game_progress(player_data, 1, 'save_data')

loaded_data = load_game_progress(1, 'save_data')

print(loaded_data)
```

In this example, the save_game_progress and load_game_progress functions accept a slot number and a file prefix, allowing for the management of multiple save slots. Each save slot is associated with a unique file, distinguished by the slot number and file prefix.

By implementing robust game session management and progress tracking, developers can create compelling gaming experiences that encourage long-term engagement and enjoyment. Players appreciate the ability to save their progress and pick up where they left off, enhancing their overall satisfaction with the game.

Saving and Loading Game States

SAVING AND LOADING game states is a crucial aspect of game development, allowing players to preserve their progress and continue their gaming experience across sessions. This process involves capturing the current state of the game, including player position, scores, inventory, and other relevant information, and then restoring this state when the game is resumed.

Game state data is typically saved to a persistent storage medium, such as files or databases, and loaded back into the game when needed. This ensures that players can pick up where they left off, even if they close the game and return later.

 # Example of saving game state to a file

```python
def save_game_state(game_state, file_path):

with open(file_path, 'w') as file:

json.dump(game_state, file)
```

 # Example of loading game state from a file

```python
def load_game_state(file_path):

with open(file_path, 'r') as file:

return json.load(file)
```

In the above code snippet, the save_game_state function saves the current game state to a file specified by file_path, while the load_game_state function loads the saved game state from the file.

Serialization

SERIALIZATION IS THE process of converting complex data structures, such as objects or dictionaries, into a format that can be easily stored or transmitted, such as JSON or XML. This allows game state data to be saved to files or databases in a structured and efficient manner.

import json

Example of serializing game state data

game_state = {

'player_position': (10, 20),

'player_health': 100,

'player_inventory': ['sword', 'shield']

}

Serialize game state to JSON

serialized_game_state = json.dumps(game_state)

print(serialized_game_state)

Deserialize game state from JSON

deserialized_game_state = json.loads(serialized_game_state)

print(deserialized_game_state)

In the code above, the json.dumps function serializes the game_state dictionary into a JSON string, while json.loads deserializes the JSON string back into a Python dictionary.

Encryption and Security

TO PROTECT SENSITIVE game data, such as player information or game progress, developers may choose to encrypt the saved game state before storing it. Encryption ensures that the data remains confidential and secure, even if the storage medium is compromised.

```python
from cryptography.fernet import Fernet

# Generate encryption key

key = Fernet.generate_key()

cipher = Fernet(key)

# Encrypt game state data

encrypted_data = cipher.encrypt(serialized_game_state.encode())

# Decrypt game state data

decrypted_data = cipher.decrypt(encrypted_data).decode()
```

In this example, the Fernet module from the cryptography library is used to generate an encryption key and encrypt the serialized game state data. The data can later be decrypted using the same key.

By implementing robust saving and loading mechanisms, developers can create games that offer a seamless and immersive experience for players, allowing them to save their progress and continue their adventures at their convenience.

Basics of AI in Gaming

ARTIFICIAL INTELLIGENCE (AI) plays a significant role in modern gaming, enhancing player experiences by providing intelligent and challenging opponents, creating dynamic game environments, and enabling sophisticated gameplay mechanics. Understanding the basics of AI in gaming is essential for game developers looking to create engaging and immersive experiences for their players.

AI in Games

IN GAMING, AI REFERS to the algorithms and systems used to simulate intelligent behavior in non-player characters (NPCs) or opponents. These algorithms enable NPCs to make decisions, react to player actions, and exhibit behaviors that mimic human intelligence. AI techniques are employed in various aspects of game development, including enemy behavior, pathfinding, decision-making, and adaptive difficulty adjustment.

 # Example of simple AI decision-making

```
def ai_decision(player_position, enemy_position):

if player_position.distance_to(enemy_position) < 10:

return "Attack"

else:

return "Move"
```

In the code snippet above, the ai_decision function determines whether an enemy NPC should attack or move based on the distance between the player and the enemy.

AI Techniques

SEVERAL AI TECHNIQUES are commonly used in gaming, each serving different purposes and contributing to the overall gameplay experience. These techniques include:

- **Finite State Machines (FSMs):** FSMs are a modeling tool used to represent the behavior of NPCs by defining a set of states and transitions between them. NPCs can switch between states based on predefined conditions, allowing for dynamic and adaptive behavior.

- **Pathfinding Algorithms:** Pathfinding algorithms are used to determine the optimal path for NPCs to navigate the game world from one point to another while avoiding obstacles. Popular pathfinding algorithms include A* (A-star) and Dijkstra's algorithm.

- **Decision Trees:** Decision trees are hierarchical structures used to model decision-making processes in NPCs. Each node in the tree represents a decision based on specific criteria, leading to different outcomes. Decision trees are commonly used for NPC behavior, quest generation, and dialogue systems.

- **Behavior Trees:** Behavior trees are a more advanced version of decision trees that allow for complex and flexible NPC behavior modeling. Behavior trees consist of nodes representing actions, conditions, and composite behaviors, enabling developers to create sophisticated AI behaviors with ease.

Challenges and Considerations

WHILE AI ENHANCES GAMING experiences, its implementation comes with various challenges and considerations. These include:

- **Performance:** AI algorithms can be computationally expensive, especially in large-scale games with many NPCs. Optimizing AI performance is essential to ensure smooth gameplay and prevent performance bottlenecks.

- **Realism:** Balancing AI behavior to provide a challenging but fair gaming experience can be challenging. NPCs should behave realistically and intelligently without appearing too predictable or unfair to players.

- **Player Experience:** AI should enhance, rather than detract from, the player experience. NPCs should provide meaningful challenges and interactions that contribute to the overall enjoyment of the game.

- **Adaptability:** AI should be adaptable to different gameplay scenarios and player actions. NPCs should react dynamically to changes in the game environment and adjust their behavior accordingly.

By mastering the basics of AI in gaming and leveraging various AI techniques and algorithms, developers can create immersive and engaging gaming experiences that captivate players and keep them coming back for more.

Implementing Pathfinding Algorithms

PATHFINDING ALGORITHMS are essential tools for creating dynamic and responsive non-player character (NPC) movement in games. These algorithms enable NPCs to navigate complex environments, avoid obstacles, and find the shortest path from one point to another. Implementing pathfinding algorithms requires an understanding of the underlying principles and considerations for optimizing performance and accuracy.

Pathfinding algorithms can be broadly categorized into two types: grid-based and graph-based. Grid-based algorithms operate on a two-dimensional grid representing the game world, while graph-based algorithms operate on a graph representing the connectivity between different points in the game world.

Grid-Based Pathfinding

GRID-BASED PATHFINDING algorithms, such as A* (A-star) and Dijkstra's algorithm, are commonly used in tile-based games where the game world is represented as a grid of cells. These algorithms work by exploring adjacent cells to find the optimal path from the starting point to the destination while considering the cost of movement and any obstacles in the way.

 # Example of A pathfinding algorithm*

```python
def astar_pathfinding(grid, start, goal):

open_set = PriorityQueue()

open_set.put(start, 0)

came_from = {}
```

```python
g_score = {cell: float('inf') for cell in grid}

g_score[start] = 0

f_score = {cell: float('inf') for cell in grid}

f_score[start] = heuristic(start, goal)

while not open_set.empty():

current = open_set.get()

if current == goal:

return reconstruct_path(came_from, goal)

for neighbor in get_neighbors(current):

tentative_g_score = g_score[current] + distance_between(current,
neighbor)

if tentative_g_score < g_score[neighbor]:

came_from[neighbor] = current

g_score[neighbor] = tentative_g_score

f_score[neighbor] = tentative_g_score + heuristic(neighbor, goal)

if neighbor not in open_set:

open_set.put(neighbor, f_score[neighbor])
```

In the code snippet above, the A* algorithm is implemented using a priority queue to explore cells in order of increasing estimated cost.

Graph-Based Pathfinding

GRAPH-BASED PATHFINDING algorithms, such as the Floyd-Warshall algorithm and the Bellman-Ford algorithm, operate on a graph representing the connectivity between different points in the game world. These algorithms are suitable for games with non-grid-based environments where movement is not restricted to discrete cells.

Graph-based pathfinding algorithms consider the edges between nodes in the graph and their associated weights to find the shortest path from the starting node to the destination.

```python
# Example of Floyd-Warshall algorithm

def floyd_warshall(graph):

distance = {}

for u in graph:

distance[u] = {}

for v in graph:

distance[u][v] = float('inf')

distance[u][u] = 0

for u in graph:

for v in graph[u]:

distance[u][v] = graph[u][v]

for k in graph:

for i in graph:
```

for j **in** graph:

distance[i][j] = min(distance[i][j], distance[i][k] + distance[k][j])

return distance

In the code snippet above, the Floyd-Warshall algorithm is used to compute the shortest paths between all pairs of nodes in the graph.

Considerations and Optimization

WHEN IMPLEMENTING PATHFINDING algorithms, developers must consider factors such as the size and complexity of the game world, the performance requirements of the game, and the accuracy and efficiency of the algorithms. Optimizing pathfinding algorithms often involves techniques such as heuristic estimation, caching, and pruning to improve performance without sacrificing accuracy.

By understanding the principles of pathfinding algorithms and their implementation, developers can create immersive and dynamic game worlds where NPCs navigate intelligently and respond to changing environments with agility and precision.

Creating Simple AI Opponents

CREATING AI OPPONENTS is a fundamental aspect of game development, especially in single-player games where players compete against computer-controlled opponents. Simple AI opponents can provide engaging gameplay experiences by simulating human-like behavior and responding dynamically to player actions.

Behavior Trees

ONE POPULAR APPROACH for creating AI opponents is using behavior trees, which are hierarchical structures that model the behavior of an AI agent as a series of sequential and parallel tasks. Behavior trees consist of nodes representing different behaviors or actions that the AI can perform, such as moving, attacking, or dodging.

```python
# Example of a basic behavior tree node

class BehaviorNode:

def __init__(self):

self.children = []

def add_child(self, child):

self.children.append(child)

def execute(self):

pass

class SequenceNode(BehaviorNode):

def execute(self):
```

```python
for child in self.children:

if not child.execute():

return False

return True

class SelectorNode(BehaviorNode):

def execute(self):

for child in self.children:

if child.execute():

return True

return False
```

In the code snippet above, BehaviorNode is a base class for all behavior tree nodes, while SequenceNode and SelectorNode are specific types of nodes used to model sequential and parallel behavior execution, respectively.

Finite State Machines

ANOTHER APPROACH FOR creating AI opponents is using finite state machines (FSMs), which model the AI's behavior as a set of discrete states and transitions between states based on predefined conditions. FSMs are useful for representing complex behaviors that can be decomposed into a finite number of states.

```python
# Example of a basic finite state machine

class State:

def __init__(self):
```

```python
    self.transitions = {}

def add_transition(self, event, next_state):
    self.transitions[event] = next_state

def on_enter(self):
    pass

def execute(self):
    pass

def on_exit(self):
    pass

class StateMachine:
    def __init__(self):
        self.states = {}
        self.current_state = None

    def add_state(self, name, state):
        self.states[name] = state

    def set_state(self, name):
        if self.current_state:
            self.current_state.on_exit()
        self.current_state = self.states[name]
        self.current_state.on_enter()
```

```python
def handle_event(self, event):

if event in self.current_state.transitions:

next_state = self.current_state.transitions[event]

self.set_state(next_state)
```

In the code snippet above, State represents an individual state in the FSM, while StateMachine manages the transitions between states based on events.

AI Behaviors and Decision Making

SIMPLE AI OPPONENTS exhibit basic behaviors such as chasing, fleeing, attacking, and evading based on the game context and player actions. These behaviors are implemented using a combination of behavior trees, FSMs, and decision-making algorithms such as rule-based systems or utility-based systems.

By combining different AI techniques and modeling behaviors using behavior trees or FSMs, developers can create AI opponents that exhibit diverse and engaging gameplay behaviors in single-player games, enhancing the overall player experience.

Advanced AI Techniques: Finite State Machines and Behavior Trees

ADVANCED AI TECHNIQUES involve the integration of various methodologies to create more sophisticated and intelligent behavior in game characters. Two common approaches are finite state machines (FSMs) and behavior trees. These techniques allow for complex decision-making processes and dynamic behavior adaptation, contributing to immersive gameplay experiences.

Combining Finite State Machines and Behavior Trees

ONE APPROACH TO ADVANCED AI development is the combination of FSMs and behavior trees. FSMs are effective for modeling state-based behavior, while behavior trees offer hierarchical organization and flexibility in decision-making. By integrating these two techniques, developers can create AI that exhibits both reactive and proactive behavior, adapting to changing game conditions.

```python
# Example of combining FSMs and behavior trees in AI development

class AIController:

def __init__(self):

self.fsm = FSM()

self.behavior_tree = BehaviorTree()

def update(self):

# Update FSM and behavior tree based on game state

self.fsm.update()
```

self.behavior_tree.execute()

In the code snippet above, the AIController class integrates both FSM and behavior tree components to control the behavior of an AI character. During the game's update loop, the FSM and behavior tree are updated to determine the AI's actions.

Dynamic Decision Making

ADVANCED AI TECHNIQUES enable dynamic decision-making based on changing environmental factors and player interactions. Through the use of decision-making algorithms such as utility theory or goal-oriented action planning, AI characters can evaluate multiple options and select the most appropriate course of action.

```python
# Example of dynamic decision-making algorithm

class UtilityAI:

def __init__(self):

self.actions = []

def add_action(self, action):

self.actions.append(action)

def select_action(self):

# Evaluate utility of each action and select the highest-scoring one

best_action = max(self.actions, key=lambda action: action.utility())

return best_action
```

In the code snippet above, the UtilityAI class implements a utility-based decision-making algorithm. Each action's utility is evaluated based on factors such as current game state, proximity to objectives, and potential rewards, allowing the AI to select the most beneficial action.

Learning and Adaptation

ADVANCED AI SYSTEMS can incorporate learning and adaptation mechanisms to improve performance over time. Techniques such as reinforcement learning, neural networks, and genetic algorithms enable AI characters to learn from experience, optimize strategies, and adapt to new challenges.

 # Example of reinforcement learning algorithm

class QLearningAgent:

def __init__(self, actions):

self.actions = actions

self.q_values = {}

def update_q_value(self, state, action, reward, next_state):

 # Update Q-value based on reward and next state

current_q_value = self.q_values.get((state, action), 0.0)

max_future_q_value = max([self.q_values.get((next_state, a), 0.0) **for** a **in** self.actions])

new_q_value = current_q_value + learning_rate * (reward + discount_factor * max_future_q_value - current_q_value)

self.q_values[(state, action)] = new_q_value

In the code snippet above, the QLearningAgent class implements the Q-learning algorithm for reinforcement learning. The agent updates its Q-values based on received rewards and estimates of future rewards, gradually improving its decision-making capabilities through trial and error.

By integrating these advanced AI techniques, developers can create game characters that exhibit human-like intelligence, adaptability, and strategic thinking, enhancing the overall gameplay experience for players.

Balancing Difficulty and AI Complexity

BALANCING THE DIFFICULTY of a game involves fine-tuning various parameters to ensure that it provides an appropriate level of challenge for players of different skill levels. Achieving this balance requires careful consideration of factors such as enemy strength, level design, resource availability, and AI complexity.

Player Skill Levels

ONE APPROACH TO DIFFICULTY balancing is to consider the range of player skill levels likely to engage with the game. By segmenting the player base into different skill categories, developers can tailor the game's challenges to suit each group. This might involve offering multiple difficulty settings or dynamically adjusting difficulty based on player performance.

```python
# Example of dynamic difficulty adjustment based on player
performance

class DifficultyManager:

def __init__(self):

self.player_skill = 0

def update_difficulty(self, player_score):

# Adjust difficulty based on player performance

if player_score > high_score_threshold:

self.player_skill = max(self.player_skill + 1, max_skill_level)

elif player_score < low_score_threshold:
```

```python
self.player_skill = max(self.player_skill - 1, min_skill_level)
```

In the code snippet above, the DifficultyManager class dynamically adjusts the game's difficulty based on the player's performance. As the player's score increases or decreases, the difficulty level is adjusted accordingly.

Enemy AI Behavior

THE BEHAVIOR OF AI-controlled opponents significantly influences the game's difficulty. Balancing AI complexity involves ensuring that enemies pose a sufficient challenge without becoming overwhelming. This might involve adjusting factors such as reaction times, decision-making logic, and combat capabilities.

```python
# Example of adjusting enemy AI difficulty

class Enemy:

def __init__(self, difficulty_level):

self.difficulty_level = difficulty_level

self.health = base_health * difficulty_level

self.attack_damage = base_damage * difficulty_level
```

In the code snippet above, the Enemy class adjusts its health and attack damage based on the game's difficulty level. Stronger enemies are spawned in higher difficulty settings, providing a greater challenge for players.

Level Design

THE LAYOUT AND STRUCTURE of game levels also contribute to overall difficulty. Balancing level design involves arranging obstacles, enemies, and rewards in a way that challenges players while still being fair and enjoyable. Developers may iterate on level designs, gathering feedback from playtesting sessions to refine difficulty curves.

Progression Systems

PROGRESSION SYSTEMS, such as experience points, upgrades, and unlocks, can impact difficulty by altering player capabilities over time. Balancing these systems involves pacing the rate of progression to align with the game's difficulty curve. Additionally, developers must ensure that progression rewards are meaningful and balanced relative to the challenges they enable players to overcome.

Community Feedback

FINALLY, COMMUNITY feedback plays a crucial role in difficulty balancing. Developers often rely on player feedback to identify areas where the game's difficulty may be too easy or too challenging. By actively engaging with the player community through forums, social media, and playtesting events, developers can gather valuable insights to inform ongoing adjustments to difficulty levels.

By carefully considering these factors and incorporating player feedback, developers can achieve a well-balanced gameplay experience that caters to a diverse audience of players. Balancing difficulty and AI complexity is an iterative process that requires continuous refinement and fine-tuning throughout the game's development lifecycle.

Got it! Let me know if you need anything else.

Chapter 11: Networking and Multiplayer Games

Understanding Basics of Network Programming in Python

NETWORKING IS A FUNDAMENTAL aspect of multiplayer game development, allowing players to interact with each other over the internet. In Python, the socket module provides a low-level interface for network communication. Sockets enable communication between different processes on the same or different machines.

To create a basic server-client architecture, you first need to understand the concepts of server and client. A server is a computer program that provides services to other computer programs or devices, known as clients. Clients initiate communication requests to servers, which then process these requests and respond accordingly.

In Python, you can create a server using the socket module. Here's a simple example of a TCP server:

import socket

 # Create a TCP/IP socket

server_socket = socket.socket(socket.AF_INET, socket.SOCK_STREAM)

 # Bind the socket to the address and port

server_address = ('localhost', 12345)

server_socket.bind(server_address)

 # Listen for incoming connections

server_socket.listen(5)

 # Accept incoming connection

client_socket, client_address = server_socket.accept()

 # Receive data from the client

data = client_socket.recv(1024)

In this code snippet, we create a TCP/IP socket, bind it to a specific address and port, and then listen for incoming connections. When a client connects to the server, the accept() method returns a new socket object and the client's address. We can then receive data from the client using the recv() method.

On the client side, you can establish a connection to the server using the following code:

import socket

 # Create a TCP/IP socket

client_socket = socket.socket(socket.AF_INET, socket.SOCK_STREAM)

 # Connect the socket to the server's address and port

server_address = ('localhost', 12345)

client_socket.connect(server_address)

 # Send data to the server

message = 'Hello, server!'

client_socket.sendall(message.encode())

This code snippet creates a TCP/IP socket and connects it to the server's address and port. It then sends a message to the server using the sendall() method.

Once the server receives the message from the client, it can process the data and send a response back to the client if necessary. This exchange of data forms the basis of network communication in multiplayer games.

Setting Up a Multiplayer Game Environment

MULTIPLAYER GAMES REQUIRE a robust networking setup to facilitate communication between players. In Python, you can use libraries like socket or higher-level frameworks like Twisted or asyncio to implement networking functionalities in your game.

When setting up a multiplayer game environment, you need to consider several key components:

1. **Server**: The server manages the game state, processes player actions, and synchronizes information between clients. It acts as the central authority in the game world.
2. **Client**: Each player connects to the server through a client application. Clients send input commands to the server and receive updates on the game state.
3. **Networking Protocol**: Define a communication protocol between the server and clients to exchange messages. This protocol should handle various aspects of gameplay, such as player movement, interactions, and synchronization.
4. **Data Serialization**: Data exchanged between the server and clients needs to be serialized for transmission over the network. Common formats include JSON, XML, or binary serialization.
5. **Game Loop Integration**: Integrate the networking functionality into your game loop to ensure smooth communication between the server and clients. Handle incoming messages, update the game state, and send updates back to the clients.

Here's a basic example of setting up a multiplayer game environment using Python's socket module:

```python
# Server

import socket

server_socket = socket.socket(socket.AF_INET,
socket.SOCK_STREAM)

server_address = ('localhost', 12345)

server_socket.bind(server_address)

server_socket.listen(5)

while True:

client_socket, client_address = server_socket.accept()

# Handle client connection

# Client

import socket

client_socket = socket.socket(socket.AF_INET,
socket.SOCK_STREAM)

server_address = ('localhost', 12345)

client_socket.connect(server_address)

# Send and receive data with the server
```

In this example, the server listens for incoming connections from clients, while the client connects to the server's address. Once connected, clients can send and receive data with the server.

Setting up a multiplayer environment involves more complexity, such as handling multiple clients, managing game sessions, and implementing game-specific networking logic. However, this basic setup forms the foundation for building multiplayer games in Python.

Synchronizing Game States Over a Network

SYNCHRONIZING GAME states between the server and clients is crucial for maintaining consistency and providing a smooth multiplayer experience. This process involves sending updates from the server to all connected clients and applying these updates to their local game states.

A common approach to synchronizing game states is through a client-server architecture:

1. **Server Authority**: The server is responsible for maintaining the authoritative game state. Clients send input commands to the server, which processes these commands and updates the game state accordingly.
2. **Delta Encoding**: To minimize bandwidth usage, only changes to the game state (delta) are transmitted from the server to clients. Instead of sending the entire game state each time, the server sends updates indicating what has changed since the last update.
3. **Client Prediction**: Clients predict the outcome of their actions locally to provide immediate feedback to players. However, the server's authoritative state overrides client predictions to prevent cheating and ensure consistency.
4. **Interpolation and Extrapolation**: Clients interpolate between received updates to smooth out movement and animation. Extrapolation can also be used to predict future positions based on current velocities.
5. **Latency Compensation**: Account for network latency by applying timestamps to updates and adjusting the game state based on the round-trip time between the client and server.

Here's a simplified example of synchronizing player movement between the server and clients:

```python
# Server

def update_player_position(player_id, new_position):

# Update player position in the server's game state

game_state[player_id]['position'] = new_position

def broadcast_state_update():

# Send updated game state to all connected clients

for client_socket in connected_clients:

client_socket.sendall(serialize(game_state))

# Client

def receive_state_update():

# Receive updated game state from the server

state_update = client_socket.recv(4096)

game_state = deserialize(state_update)

def send_player_input(input_command):

# Send player input command to the server

client_socket.sendall(serialize(input_command))
```

In this example, when a player sends input commands to the server (e.g., moving their character), the server updates the game state accordingly. It then broadcasts the updated game state to all connected clients, who apply the changes to their local game states.

This ensures that all players see the same game world and experience synchronized gameplay.

Handling Latency and Network Issues

LATENCY, OR THE DELAY between sending a packet and receiving a response, is a common challenge in networked multiplayer games. Dealing with latency is crucial for ensuring smooth gameplay and preventing issues like lag and desync. Here are some techniques used to handle latency and other network issues:

1. **Prediction and Reconciliation**: Predictive algorithms are used to estimate the outcome of player actions before receiving confirmation from the server. Clients predict the results of their actions locally and then reconcile any differences with the authoritative server state upon receiving updates. This helps in maintaining smooth gameplay even in the presence of latency.

2. **Interpolation and Extrapolation**: Interpolation involves smoothing out movement between received updates to reduce the perception of jittery movement caused by packet loss or latency. Extrapolation predicts future positions based on current velocities to compensate for latency and ensure smoother animation.

3. **Client-Side Prediction**: Client-side prediction allows players to interact with the game world without waiting for server validation. However, the server ultimately overrides client predictions to maintain consistency and prevent cheating.

4. **Dead Reckoning**: Dead reckoning is a technique where clients predict the movement of objects based on their last known state and velocity. This helps in reducing the impact of latency on object movement, especially in fast-paced games.

5. **Bandwidth Optimization**: Minimizing the amount of

data transmitted between clients and servers helps in reducing latency and network congestion. Techniques such as delta encoding and compression are used to optimize network traffic.

6. **Network Interpolation Delay**: Adding a small delay before applying received updates helps in smoothing out network jitter and reducing the impact of sudden changes in latency. However, excessive delay can lead to perceived sluggishness in gameplay.

7. **Server-Side Lag Compensation**: Lag compensation techniques adjust the game state on the server to account for network latency. This ensures that actions performed by players are accurately reflected in the game world, even if there is a delay between input and execution.

8. **Client-Side Lag Indicators**: Providing visual or auditory cues to players indicating network latency helps in managing player expectations and reducing frustration. These indicators can alert players when their actions are experiencing delays due to network issues.

Overall, handling latency and network issues is a critical aspect of multiplayer game development. By implementing appropriate techniques and optimizations, developers can create multiplayer experiences that are enjoyable and responsive for players, even under challenging network conditions.

Designing and Implementing Online Game Lobbies

ONLINE GAME LOBBIES play a crucial role in facilitating multiplayer gaming experiences by allowing players to connect, interact, and organize game sessions. Here are some key considerations for designing and implementing effective online game lobbies:

1. **User Interface Design**: The user interface (UI) of the lobby should be intuitive and visually appealing, making it easy for players to navigate and interact with different features. Clear labels, descriptive icons, and logical layout contribute to a seamless user experience.

2. **Authentication and Authorization**: Implement secure authentication mechanisms to verify the identity of players and ensure that only authorized users can access the lobby. Techniques such as OAuth or token-based authentication can be used to protect against unauthorized access.

3. **Player Matching and Searching**: Provide features for players to search and filter available game sessions based on criteria such as game mode, skill level, region, and player count. Efficient matchmaking algorithms help in pairing players with compatible opponents or teammates.

4. **Chat and Communication**: Integration of real-time chat functionality allows players to communicate with each other before, during, and after game sessions. Features like private messaging, group chat, and voice chat enhance social interaction and coordination among players.

5. **Game Session Management**: The lobby should support the creation, joining, and management of game sessions. Players should be able to host private or public game

sessions, invite friends, and configure game settings such as map selection, game mode, and match duration.

6. **Player Profiles and Statistics**: Displaying player profiles with relevant statistics, achievements, and progress enhances player engagement and provides a sense of accomplishment. Leaderboards and ranking systems can also encourage healthy competition among players.

7. **Customization and Personalization**: Allow players to customize their avatars, usernames, and other profile details to reflect their personality and preferences. Personalization options contribute to a sense of identity and ownership within the game community.

8. **Notification and Alerts**: Implement notification systems to inform players about important events such as new game sessions, friend requests, or system updates. Timely alerts keep players informed and engaged even when they are not actively using the lobby.

9. **Scalability and Performance**: Design the lobby system to handle large numbers of concurrent users without sacrificing performance or responsiveness. Scalable architecture, efficient data storage, and load balancing techniques are essential for handling peak traffic loads.

10. **Security and Privacy**: Protect player data and privacy by implementing robust security measures such as encryption, data validation, and access controls. Compliance with regulations such as GDPR ensures that player information is handled responsibly and ethically.

11. **Feedback and Iteration**: Gather feedback from players and iterate on the lobby design based on user suggestions, usability tests, and analytics data. Continuous improvement ensures that the lobby meets the evolving needs and expectations of the player community.

By focusing on these key aspects, developers can create online game lobbies that provide a seamless and enjoyable experience for players, fostering community engagement and long-term retention.

Optimization and Performance

Analyzing and Improving Game Performance

OPTIMIZING GAME PERFORMANCE is essential for delivering a smooth and enjoyable gaming experience to players. In this section, we'll explore various techniques for analyzing and improving game performance.

Profiling Tools: Profiling tools help identify performance bottlenecks in your game code by measuring the execution time of different functions and sections. Tools like cProfile for Python or built-in profilers in IDEs can provide valuable insights into which parts of your code are consuming the most resources.

Frame Rate Monitoring: Monitoring the frame rate of your game allows you to assess its performance in real-time. Consistently achieving a high frame rate, ideally 60 frames per second (FPS) or higher, ensures smooth gameplay and responsiveness. Frame rate drops or fluctuations indicate performance issues that need to be addressed.

Graphics Optimization: Optimizing graphics rendering is crucial for improving performance, especially in graphically intensive games. Techniques such as level-of-detail (LOD) rendering, occlusion culling, and batching reduce the number of draw calls and polygons rendered, resulting in faster frame rates.

Asset Compression: Compressing game assets such as textures, audio files, and models reduces their file size and memory footprint, improving loading times and runtime performance. Utilize compression formats like PNG, JPEG, or OGG for assets while maintaining acceptable quality.

Memory Management: Efficient memory management is essential for preventing memory leaks and excessive memory usage. Use data structures and algorithms that minimize memory overhead, and release resources promptly when they are no longer needed. Avoid unnecessary object creation and destruction to reduce garbage collection overhead.

CPU and GPU Optimization: Optimize CPU and GPU usage by minimizing unnecessary calculations and rendering operations. Use efficient algorithms, data structures, and rendering techniques to maximize hardware utilization while minimizing overhead. Profile and optimize hotspots in your code to reduce CPU and GPU load.

Multithreading and Parallelism: Leveraging multithreading and parallelism can improve performance by distributing computational tasks across multiple CPU cores. Offload non-blocking or CPU-intensive tasks such as pathfinding, AI calculations, and physics simulations to separate threads to maximize CPU utilization.

Caching and Preloading: Cache frequently accessed data and pre-load resources during the game's initialization phase to reduce loading times and improve runtime performance. Use techniques like texture atlases, object pooling, and resource bundling to minimize loading overhead during gameplay.

Code Optimization: Optimize critical sections of your code by minimizing redundant calculations, loop iterations, and function calls. Use efficient algorithms and data structures tailored to your specific requirements to reduce computational complexity and improve overall performance.

Continuous Testing and Profiling: Continuously test and profile your game throughout the development process to identify and address performance issues early. Regular profiling sessions help track performance improvements and ensure that the game meets its performance targets across different platforms and hardware configurations.

By implementing these optimization techniques and prioritizing performance throughout the development cycle, you can create games that deliver smooth and responsive gameplay experiences, enhancing player satisfaction and engagement.

Managing Game Resources Efficiently

EFFICIENT MANAGEMENT of game resources is crucial for optimizing performance and ensuring a smooth gaming experience. In this section, we'll discuss various strategies for managing resources effectively.

Resource Loading: Load game resources, such as textures, audio files, and level data, asynchronously to minimize loading times and avoid blocking the main thread. Utilize background loading techniques to fetch resources while the game is running, ensuring seamless gameplay transitions.

Resource Caching: Implement a caching mechanism to store frequently used resources in memory, reducing the need for repeated loading from disk. Cache textures, sound effects, and other assets to improve runtime performance and responsiveness. Use least recently used (LRU) or time-based cache eviction policies to manage cache size and prevent memory overflow.

Resource Pooling: Pooling reusable game objects, such as projectiles, enemies, and particles, reduces memory allocation overhead and improves performance. Create object pools for frequently instantiated objects and reuse them instead of creating new instances. Implement pooling for both static and dynamic objects to optimize memory usage and garbage collection overhead.

Texture Atlas: Combine multiple textures into a single texture atlas to minimize texture switching and reduce draw call overhead. Pack spritesheets and texture maps into a single image file and use texture coordinates to render individual sprites. Texture atlases improve rendering performance by reducing the number of texture binds and state changes.

Audio Streaming: Stream large audio files, such as background music and ambient sounds, from disk or memory to minimize memory usage and loading times. Use streaming audio formats like OGG or MP3 to play audio files directly from disk, loading only the portions needed for playback. Implement buffering and caching to ensure smooth streaming and uninterrupted playback.

Level Streaming: Divide large game levels into smaller chunks and stream them dynamically based on the player's position and visibility. Load and unload level segments as needed to conserve memory and reduce loading times. Implement level streaming systems that prioritize loading nearby areas while unloading distant or occluded regions to optimize resource usage.

Dynamic Resource Loading: Dynamically load and unload resources based on gameplay events, such as entering a new area, completing a level, or triggering scripted events. Load assets on-demand to minimize memory overhead and improve runtime performance. Implement resource management systems that track resource dependencies and unload unused assets to free up memory.

Resource Compression: Compress game assets, such as textures, audio files, and level data, to reduce storage requirements and loading times. Use lossless or lossy compression algorithms like PNG, JPEG, OGG, or LZMA to compress assets without sacrificing quality. Balance compression ratio with decompression overhead to achieve optimal performance.

Resource Optimization Tools: Utilize asset optimization tools and pipelines to automate resource compression, packaging, and management tasks. Use tools like texture compressors, audio encoders, and level optimizers to preprocess assets and generate optimized versions for deployment. Integrate asset optimization into your build process to streamline development and improve workflow efficiency.

Memory Profiling: Profile memory usage during runtime to identify memory leaks, excessive allocations, and inefficient resource usage patterns. Use memory profiling tools and profilers to monitor memory allocation, usage, and fragmentation in real-time. Analyze memory snapshots and allocation patterns to optimize resource usage and minimize memory overhead.

By implementing these resource management strategies and techniques, you can optimize memory usage, reduce loading times, and improve overall performance in your games. Efficient resource management ensures that your game runs smoothly across different platforms and hardware configurations, enhancing player satisfaction and engagement.

Techniques for Reducing Lag and Improving FPS

REDUCING LAG AND IMPROVING FPS (frames per second) are essential for delivering a smooth and responsive gaming experience. In this section, we'll explore various techniques to achieve these goals.

Optimized Rendering: Optimize rendering performance by minimizing the number of draw calls, reducing overdraw, and using hardware-accelerated rendering techniques. Batch rendering operations, group objects with similar properties, and minimize state changes to improve rendering efficiency. Utilize hardware features like instancing, vertex buffer objects (VBOs), and indexed rendering to reduce CPU overhead and improve GPU performance.

Level of Detail (LOD): Implement LOD systems to dynamically adjust the level of detail based on the distance from the camera. Use simplified meshes, lower-resolution textures, and fewer polygons for distant objects to reduce rendering complexity and improve performance. Gradually increase detail as objects move closer to the camera to maintain visual quality while optimizing performance.

Culling Techniques: Implement frustum culling, occlusion culling, and visibility culling to eliminate unnecessary rendering of objects outside the view frustum or occluded by other geometry. Use spatial partitioning data structures like octrees, quad trees, or bounding volume hierarchies (BVH) to efficiently cull objects and optimize rendering. Implement efficient culling algorithms that minimize CPU overhead and maximize culling accuracy.

Dynamic Batched Rendering: Dynamically batch renderable objects, such as sprites, meshes, and particles, into fewer draw calls to reduce CPU overhead and improve rendering performance. Group objects with similar properties, such as materials, shaders, and textures, into batches and render them together using instancing or hardware features like geometry shaders. Use dynamic batching techniques to combine smaller objects into larger batches at runtime, reducing draw call overhead and improving performance.

Asynchronous Loading and Streaming: Load game assets asynchronously and stream resources dynamically to minimize loading times and avoid blocking the main thread. Use background loading techniques to fetch resources from disk or memory while the game is running, ensuring smooth gameplay transitions and uninterrupted performance. Implement streaming systems for large assets like textures, audio files, and level data to load and unload them on-the-fly based on player position and visibility.

CPU and GPU Optimization: Optimize CPU and GPU performance by reducing unnecessary computations, minimizing memory bandwidth usage, and optimizing algorithms and data structures. Profile performance using CPU and GPU profilers to identify bottlenecks and optimize critical code paths. Utilize multi-threading, SIMD instructions, and parallel processing techniques to distribute computational workload and maximize CPU utilization. Optimize GPU shaders, texture formats, and rendering techniques to minimize GPU rendering time and improve frame rate.

Frame Rate Regulation: Implement frame rate regulation techniques, such as vertical synchronization (V-Sync), frame rate capping, and adaptive frame rate control, to maintain consistent frame rates and prevent screen tearing and stuttering. Use platform-specific APIs and settings to synchronize rendering with display refresh rates and limit frame rate fluctuations. Implement adaptive frame rate control algorithms that dynamically adjust rendering quality and detail based on system performance and user preferences.

Memory Management: Efficient memory management is crucial for reducing lag and improving FPS. Minimize memory allocations, avoid memory leaks, and optimize memory usage to prevent excessive garbage collection and reduce memory fragmentation. Use object pooling, resource caching, and memory profiling tools to optimize memory usage and improve runtime performance. Analyze memory allocation patterns and optimize data structures and algorithms to minimize memory overhead and improve cache locality.

Platform-specific Optimization: Implement platform-specific optimizations for different hardware configurations, operating systems, and target platforms. Utilize platform-specific APIs, hardware features, and performance tuning techniques to maximize performance and compatibility. Optimize graphics settings, audio configurations, and input processing for specific platforms to ensure optimal performance and user experience.

By applying these techniques and best practices, you can significantly reduce lag, improve FPS, and deliver a smooth and responsive gaming experience across a wide range of platforms and hardware configurations. Optimal performance is essential for engaging gameplay and player satisfaction, making performance optimization a critical aspect of game development.

Profiling and Debugging Pygame Applications

PROFILING AND DEBUGGING are essential processes in game development for identifying performance bottlenecks, optimizing code, and fixing bugs. In this section, we'll explore various techniques and tools for profiling and debugging Pygame applications.

Profiling Tools: Use profiling tools to analyze the performance of Pygame applications and identify areas for optimization. Profilers gather data on CPU usage, memory usage, function call times, and other performance metrics to help developers understand where time is spent during execution. Popular Python profilers include cProfile, line_profiler, and memory_profiler, which provide insights into code execution and memory usage.

Performance Analysis: Perform performance analysis using profilers to identify performance bottlenecks and optimize critical code paths. Profile the entire application or specific modules to measure CPU and memory usage, identify hotspots, and prioritize optimization efforts. Analyze profiling data to understand which functions or code blocks consume the most resources and where optimizations can be applied effectively.

Optimization Strategies: Apply optimization strategies based on profiling data to improve the performance of Pygame applications. Optimize algorithms, data structures, and computational complexity to reduce CPU overhead and improve frame rate. Minimize memory allocations, eliminate unnecessary computations, and optimize rendering and physics calculations to enhance overall performance. Profile optimized code to measure performance gains and validate optimization efforts.

Debugging Tools: Use debugging tools to identify and fix bugs, errors, and unexpected behavior in Pygame applications. Debuggers provide features for stepping through code, inspecting variables, setting breakpoints, and analyzing program state during runtime. Pygame developers can use integrated development environments (IDEs) like PyCharm, Visual Studio Code, or debuggers like pdb and PyDev for debugging Python code and troubleshooting issues.

Error Handling and Logging: Implement error handling and logging mechanisms to capture errors, exceptions, and runtime issues in Pygame applications. Use try-except blocks, assertions, and logging libraries like Python's logging module to handle errors gracefully and provide useful feedback to developers and users. Log messages, warnings, and errors to files or consoles to diagnose problems, track down bugs, and monitor application behavior.

Unit Testing: Write unit tests to verify the correctness of Pygame code and ensure that individual components function as expected. Use Python's built-in unittest framework or third-party testing libraries like pytest to create automated tests for Pygame modules, classes, and functions. Write test cases to cover different use cases, edge cases, and error conditions, and run tests regularly to validate code changes and prevent regressions.

Integration Testing: Perform integration testing to validate the behavior and interaction of multiple components within Pygame applications. Test integrated systems, modules, and features to ensure that they work together correctly and produce the desired results. Use test suites, test runners, and continuous integration (CI) tools to automate integration testing and verify the overall functionality and stability of Pygame applications.

Performance Profiling: Profile Pygame applications for performance optimization by measuring frame rate, rendering time, and other performance metrics. Use built-in profiling tools like pygame.time.Clock to measure frame rate and pygame.time.get_ticks to measure elapsed time. Profile rendering performance using pygame.display.update and pygame.display.flip to identify rendering bottlenecks and optimize frame rendering.

Memory Profiling: Profile memory usage in Pygame applications to identify memory leaks, excessive allocations, and inefficient memory usage patterns. Use memory_profiler or other memory profiling tools to track memory allocation, deallocation, and usage over time. Profile memory-intensive operations like loading images, creating surfaces, and allocating resources to identify areas for memory optimization and improvement.

Optimization Tips: Apply optimization tips and best practices to improve the performance and efficiency of Pygame applications. Optimize rendering by minimizing overdraw, reducing the number of draw calls, and using hardware-accelerated rendering techniques. Optimize input handling, event processing, and update logic to minimize CPU overhead and improve frame rate. Profile and optimize critical code paths, algorithms, and data structures to maximize performance and responsiveness.

By leveraging profiling and debugging techniques, Pygame developers can identify performance bottlenecks, optimize code, and deliver high-quality games with smooth gameplay, responsive controls, and optimal performance. Profiling and debugging are essential aspects of game development that help ensure the stability, reliability, and performance of Pygame applications.

Scaling Games for Different Hardware

SCALING GAMES FOR DIFFERENT hardware configurations is crucial to ensure optimal performance and user experience across a wide range of devices. In this section, we'll explore strategies for scaling Pygame games to accommodate various hardware specifications and capabilities.

Hardware Considerations: Consider the hardware specifications and capabilities of target devices when developing and scaling Pygame games. Take into account factors such as CPU speed, RAM size, GPU performance, screen resolution, and input devices when optimizing games for different platforms and hardware configurations. Test games on a variety of devices to identify performance bottlenecks and compatibility issues and adjust settings accordingly.

Performance Optimization: Optimize Pygame games for performance to ensure smooth gameplay and responsiveness on different hardware platforms. Profile and optimize critical code paths, rendering operations, and resource usage to minimize CPU and memory overhead. Use hardware-accelerated rendering techniques, efficient algorithms, and optimized data structures to maximize performance and frame rate on low-end devices.

Resolution Scaling: Implement resolution scaling to adapt Pygame games to different screen resolutions and aspect ratios. Use techniques like letterboxing, pillarboxing, or stretching to maintain the correct aspect ratio and display games properly on screens with different dimensions. Adjust rendering parameters, viewport size, and scaling factors dynamically based on the target device's screen resolution to optimize graphics quality and performance.

Graphics Settings: Provide customizable graphics settings in Pygame games to allow users to adjust visual quality and performance according to their hardware capabilities. Offer options for adjusting resolution, texture quality, anti-aliasing, shadow quality, and other graphical effects to balance performance and visual fidelity. Allow users to disable or enable specific features based on their preferences and hardware limitations.

Input Configuration: Support different input devices and control schemes in Pygame games to accommodate various hardware configurations. Provide options for configuring keyboard, mouse, gamepad, touchscreen, and other input devices to cater to different player preferences and accessibility needs. Implement customizable key bindings, sensitivity settings, and input mappings to ensure smooth and intuitive controls across different devices.

Platform Compatibility: Ensure compatibility with different operating systems, hardware platforms, and Pygame versions when scaling games for different hardware configurations. Test games on multiple platforms, including Windows, macOS, Linux, Android, iOS, and web browsers, to identify platform-specific issues and ensure cross-platform compatibility. Follow best practices for platform-specific development and deployment to maximize compatibility and performance.

Performance Profiling: Profile Pygame games on target hardware to identify performance bottlenecks and optimize resource usage. Use profiling tools and performance monitoring utilities to measure CPU and memory usage, frame rate, rendering time, and other performance metrics on different devices. Analyze profiling data to identify areas for optimization and prioritize performance improvements based on hardware limitations and user experience requirements.

User Feedback: Gather feedback from users to understand performance issues and hardware compatibility problems experienced on different devices. Encourage players to report performance-related issues, bugs, and compatibility issues encountered during gameplay. Use user feedback to prioritize bug fixes, performance optimizations, and hardware compatibility updates in future game releases.

Continuous Optimization: Continuously optimize and update Pygame games to address performance issues, compatibility problems, and hardware limitations over time. Monitor performance metrics, user feedback, and hardware trends to identify emerging issues and opportunities for improvement. Release regular updates, patches, and optimizations to enhance game performance, compatibility, and user experience on different hardware configurations.

By following these scaling strategies and best practices, Pygame developers can ensure that their games deliver optimal performance and user experience across a wide range of hardware configurations and platforms. Scaling games effectively for different hardware enables developers to reach a broader audience and maximize the impact and accessibility of their Pygame creations.

Chapter 13: Packaging and Distribution

Preparing Your Game for Distribution

PREPARING A PYGAME game for distribution involves several important steps to ensure that it can be packaged and distributed effectively to players. In this section, we'll explore the process of preparing a Pygame game for distribution, including optimizing assets, bundling dependencies, and creating distributable packages.

Asset Optimization: Before packaging a Pygame game for distribution, it's essential to optimize game assets such as images, sounds, and fonts to reduce file size and improve loading times. Use compression techniques, image optimization tools, and audio compression algorithms to minimize the size of assets without compromising quality. Convert assets to optimized formats and resolutions suitable for the target platform and screen resolution to enhance performance and reduce storage requirements.

Dependency Management: Identify and bundle dependencies required by the Pygame game to ensure that it runs smoothly on target devices without additional installation steps. Package external libraries, modules, and resources used by the game alongside the main executable or game files to simplify deployment and minimize compatibility issues. Include license information, attribution credits, and copyright notices for bundled dependencies to comply with licensing requirements and legal obligations.

Executable Packaging: Package Pygame games as standalone executables or installer packages for easy distribution and installation on target platforms. Use tools like PyInstaller, cx_Freeze, or py2exe to bundle Python scripts, dependencies, and assets into standalone executables compatible with Windows, macOS, Linux, and other operating systems. Customize packaging options, file paths, and distribution settings to optimize performance, security, and user experience on different platforms.

Versioning and Release Management: Adopt versioning and release management practices to track changes, updates, and releases of Pygame games over time. Assign version numbers, release dates, and release notes to each game release to communicate changes, improvements, and bug fixes to players. Follow a structured release cycle, such as semantic versioning, to indicate the significance of updates and ensure compatibility with existing installations and saved games.

Platform-specific Considerations: Consider platform-specific requirements, guidelines, and restrictions when preparing Pygame games for distribution on different platforms. Adhere to platform-specific packaging and distribution standards, such as Windows Installer (MSI), macOS Disk Image (DMG), or Linux package formats (DEB, RPM), to ensure compatibility and compliance with platform policies and security measures. Test packaged games on target platforms to verify functionality, performance, and user experience across different operating systems and hardware configurations.

Digital Signing and Certification: Sign and certify packaged Pygame games with digital signatures and certificates to verify their authenticity and integrity and establish trust with players and users. Obtain code signing certificates from trusted certificate authorities (CAs) and sign executable files and installer packages to prevent tampering, malware injection, and unauthorized modifications. Include digital signatures and certificate information in packaged games to reassure players and comply with security requirements on supported platforms.

Distribution Channels: Choose appropriate distribution channels and platforms to publish and distribute Pygame games to a wide audience of players. Explore online marketplaces, app stores, game distribution platforms, and community forums to promote and distribute games to potential players and fans. Consider publishing games on platforms like Steam, itch.io, Google Play, Apple App Store, or GitHub to reach diverse audiences and maximize visibility, discoverability, and monetization opportunities.

Documentation and Support: Provide comprehensive documentation, tutorials, and support resources to help players install, configure, and troubleshoot Pygame games on different platforms and devices. Create user manuals, setup guides, troubleshooting FAQs, and community forums to address common issues, questions, and feedback from players. Offer timely customer support, bug fixes, and updates to ensure a positive user experience and foster a supportive community of players and fans.

Legal Compliance: Ensure legal compliance and intellectual property protection when packaging and distributing Pygame games to avoid copyright infringement, licensing violations, and legal disputes. Obtain necessary permissions, licenses, and rights for third-party assets, intellectual property, and content used in the game, including graphics, music, sound effects, fonts, and trademarks. Clearly communicate terms of use, end-user license agreements (EULAs), and privacy policies to players and users to establish legal agreements and protect developer rights and interests.

Marketing and Promotion: Develop marketing strategies and promotional campaigns to increase awareness, visibility, and adoption of Pygame games among target audiences and communities. Create compelling trailers, screenshots, gameplay footage, and promotional materials to showcase the features, gameplay, and unique selling points of the game. Engage with influencers, streamers, press outlets, and social media channels to generate buzz, reviews, and word-of-mouth recommendations for the game. Participate in game jams, festivals, conventions, and industry events to network with developers, showcase games, and build relationships with players and fans.

By following these preparation steps and best practices, Pygame developers can effectively package and distribute their games to players worldwide, reach broader audiences, and maximize the success and impact of their creations. Effective packaging and distribution are essential components of the game development process, enabling developers to share their passion, creativity, and vision with the world and create memorable gaming experiences for players of all ages and backgrounds.

Creating Executable Files for Windows, Mac, and Linux

CREATING EXECUTABLE files for different operating systems is a crucial step in packaging and distributing Pygame games to players. Each platform has its own requirements and tools for generating executable files that can run standalone without the need for Python or Pygame installations. In this section, we'll explore the process of creating executable files for Windows, Mac, and Linux platforms.

Windows: On Windows, Pygame developers can use tools like PyInstaller or cx_Freeze to create standalone executable files (EXE) from Python scripts. PyInstaller is a popular choice for packaging Python applications into single EXE files along with necessary dependencies and assets. Developers can install PyInstaller using pip and then use it to generate an EXE file for their Pygame game by running a command in the terminal or command prompt. PyInstaller automatically detects dependencies and bundles them into the EXE file, making it easy to distribute and run on Windows systems without requiring Python or Pygame installations.

Mac: On macOS, Pygame developers can use similar tools like PyInstaller or cx_Freeze to create standalone application bundles (APP) that can be distributed and run on Mac systems. PyInstaller supports macOS and can generate APP bundles from Python scripts with dependencies and assets. Developers can install PyInstaller using pip and then use it to package their Pygame game into an APP bundle by running a command in the terminal. PyInstaller handles the bundling of dependencies and resources into the APP bundle, allowing users to run the game on macOS without Python or Pygame installations.

Linux: On Linux, Pygame developers can use PyInstaller, cx_Freeze, or other tools to create executable files or distribution packages (DEB, RPM) for different Linux distributions. PyInstaller supports Linux and can generate standalone executable files or distribution packages from Python scripts. Developers can install PyInstaller using pip and then use it to package their Pygame game into an executable file or distribution package by running a command in the terminal. PyInstaller includes options for customizing packaging settings and handling dependencies to ensure compatibility and ease of installation on Linux systems.

Cross-platform Packaging: To simplify cross-platform packaging and distribution of Pygame games, developers can use platform-independent packaging formats like ZIP or TAR archives. By bundling Python scripts, assets, and dependencies into a single archive file, developers can distribute their games to players on different platforms without the need for platform-specific executable files or installation procedures. Players can extract the archive and run the game directly from the extracted files, making it convenient to play games on any supported platform without additional steps or requirements.

Testing and Validation: After creating executable files or distribution packages for different platforms, it's essential to test and validate them on target systems to ensure compatibility, functionality, and performance. Developers should test their packaged games on various versions of Windows, macOS, and Linux to identify and address platform-specific issues, bugs, and compatibility issues. Conduct thorough testing on different hardware configurations, screen resolutions, and system configurations to verify that the game runs smoothly and meets quality standards on all supported platforms.

Distribution Channels: Once executable files or distribution packages are created and tested, developers can distribute their Pygame games through various channels and platforms to reach a wide audience of players. Consider publishing games on online marketplaces, app stores, game distribution platforms, and community forums to promote and distribute games to potential players and fans. Provide clear instructions, download links, and installation guides to help players download, install, and play the game on their preferred platform.

Documentation and Support: Provide comprehensive documentation, tutorials, and support resources to help players download, install, and run Pygame games on different platforms. Create platform-specific setup guides, troubleshooting FAQs, and community forums to address common issues, questions, and feedback from players. Offer timely customer support, bug fixes, and updates to ensure a positive user experience and foster a supportive community of players and fans across all supported platforms.

Legal Compliance: Ensure legal compliance and intellectual property protection when packaging and distributing Pygame games to avoid copyright infringement, licensing violations, and legal disputes. Obtain necessary permissions, licenses, and rights for third-party assets, intellectual property, and content used in the game, including graphics, music, sound effects, fonts, and trademarks. Clearly communicate terms of use, end-user license agreements (EULAs), and privacy policies to players and users to establish legal agreements and protect developer rights and interests.

By following these steps and best practices, Pygame developers can effectively create executable files for Windows, Mac, and Linux platforms, package and distribute their games to players worldwide, and maximize the reach and impact of their creations. Effective packaging and distribution are essential components of the game development process, enabling developers to share their passion, creativity, and vision with players on different platforms and devices.

Distributing Through Online Platforms

DISTRIBUTING PYGAME games through online platforms is a popular and effective way to reach a broad audience of players and potential fans. Online platforms provide developers with access to large user bases, built-in distribution channels, and marketing opportunities to promote and showcase their games to a global audience. In this section, we'll explore various online platforms and distribution channels that Pygame developers can leverage to distribute their games and connect with players worldwide.

Steam: Steam is one of the largest and most popular digital distribution platforms for PC games, offering a vast library of games, community features, and developer tools for publishing and selling games. Pygame developers can publish their games on Steam through the Steamworks developer portal, where they can set up store pages, upload game builds, and manage game releases, updates, and promotional activities. Steam provides access to a massive user base of millions of players worldwide, along with features like user reviews, forums, achievements, and multiplayer matchmaking to engage and interact with players.

itch.io: itch.io is a versatile and developer-friendly platform that allows independent game developers to publish, sell, and distribute their games online. Pygame developers can create game pages on itch.io, where they can upload game builds, set pricing options, and customize storefronts with screenshots, trailers, and descriptions to attract players. itch.io supports various payment models, including pay-what-you-want, free downloads, and commercial sales, giving developers flexibility in monetizing their games. Additionally, itch.io provides features like analytics, community forums, and game jams to support developers and connect them with players and collaborators.

Game Jolt: Game Jolt is a vibrant and community-driven platform that hosts indie games, game jams, and development tools for game creators. Pygame developers can upload their games to Game Jolt, where they can create game pages, share updates, and interact with players through comments, ratings, and feedback. Game Jolt supports various monetization options, including ad revenue sharing, donations, and direct sales, allowing developers to earn revenue from their games. Additionally, Game Jolt hosts regular game jams and contests to encourage creativity and collaboration among developers and provide exposure to new and innovative games.

Google Play Store: For mobile game developers targeting Android devices, the Google Play Store is a primary distribution platform for publishing and promoting games to millions of Android users worldwide. Pygame developers can package their games as Android apps using tools like Pygame Subset for Android (PGS4A) or Kivy and publish them on the Google Play Store through the Google Play Console developer portal. By optimizing their game listings with compelling visuals, descriptions, and keywords, developers can improve discoverability and attract users to download and play their games on Android smartphones and tablets.

Apple App Store: For iOS game developers targeting iPhone and iPad users, the Apple App Store is a leading platform for distributing and monetizing games on iOS devices. Pygame developers can package their games as iOS apps using tools like Pygame Subset for iOS (PGS4A) or Kivy and submit them to the App Store through the App Store Connect developer portal. Apple provides tools and guidelines for app submission, review, and approval, ensuring that published games meet quality standards and comply with App Store policies. By leveraging features like in-app purchases, subscriptions, and app store optimization (ASO), developers can maximize revenue and user engagement on the App Store.

Web Platforms: In addition to native app stores, Pygame developers can distribute their games on web platforms and portals to reach players directly through web browsers. By exporting games as HTML5 applications using tools like Pygame to JavaScript compilers or web frameworks like Pygame Zero, developers can host their games on websites, shareable URLs, or game portals like Kongregate, Newgrounds, or Game Jolt. Web platforms provide instant access to games without the need for downloads or installations, making them accessible to a broad audience of players across different devices and platforms.

Social Media and Communities: Beyond traditional distribution platforms, Pygame developers can leverage social media channels, online communities, and game forums to promote and share their games with players and fans. By engaging with communities on platforms like Reddit, Twitter, Facebook, and Discord, developers can build relationships, gather feedback, and generate buzz around their games through posts, screenshots, trailers, and livestreams. Participating in relevant forums, subreddits, and Discord servers allows developers to connect with players who share common interests and preferences, fostering a supportive community around their games.

Crowdfunding and Preorders: To fund game development and generate early interest, Pygame developers can utilize crowdfunding platforms like Kickstarter, IndieGoGo, or Patreon to launch crowdfunding campaigns or offer preorder incentives to backers and supporters. Crowdfunding campaigns allow developers to showcase their games, set funding goals, and offer rewards to backers in exchange for pledges, providing financial support and community engagement throughout the development process. Preorder campaigns enable developers to offer early access to games, exclusive content, and limited-time discounts to players who preorder the game before its official release, generating revenue and building anticipation for the game's launch.

Analytics and Performance Tracking: When distributing games through online platforms, it's essential for developers to track performance metrics, analytics, and user engagement data to evaluate the success of their distribution efforts and make informed decisions for future updates and marketing strategies. By using analytics tools like Google Analytics, Steamworks Stats, or itch.io's

Marketing Your Game

MARKETING PLAYS A CRUCIAL role in the success of a game, helping developers attract players, generate interest, and drive sales. In this section, we'll explore various marketing strategies and techniques that Pygame developers can use to promote their games effectively and maximize their visibility and reach.

Establishing an Online Presence: Building a strong online presence is essential for reaching potential players and connecting with the gaming community. Pygame developers can create dedicated websites, blogs, or social media profiles for their games to showcase development progress, share updates, and engage with fans and followers. By regularly posting content like devlogs, gameplay videos, and screenshots, developers can keep their audience informed and excited about their game's development journey.

Creating Compelling Visuals: Visual assets such as trailers, screenshots, and promotional artwork play a significant role in capturing players' attention and conveying the essence of a game. Pygame developers should invest time in creating high-quality visuals that highlight the unique features, art style, and gameplay mechanics of their games. Eye-catching trailers, vibrant screenshots, and captivating artwork can pique players' interest and encourage them to learn more about the game.

Utilizing Social Media Platforms: Social media platforms like Twitter, Facebook, Instagram, and TikTok provide valuable opportunities for promoting games and engaging with potential players. Pygame developers can leverage these platforms to share updates, announce milestones, and interact with their audience through posts, stories, and live streams. By using hashtags, mentions, and relevant communities, developers can expand their reach and attract attention to their games within the gaming community and beyond.

Engaging with Influencers and Content Creators: Collaborating with influencers, streamers, and content creators can significantly amplify a game's exposure and reach a wider audience. Pygame developers can reach out to YouTubers, Twitch streamers, and social media influencers who create content related to indie games, retro gaming, or game development. By providing review copies, access to early builds, or sponsored content opportunities, developers can encourage influencers to play and promote their games to their followers, generating buzz and driving traffic to their game's store page.

Participating in Game Jams and Events: Game jams and indie game events are excellent opportunities for developers to showcase their games, network with industry professionals, and build relationships with players and fellow developers. Pygame developers can participate in online and offline game jams like Ludum Dare, Global Game Jam, or PyWeek to create and share game prototypes within a limited timeframe. Additionally, attending gaming conventions, conferences, and expos allows developers to demo their games, gather feedback, and connect with potential collaborators, publishers, and press outlets.

Optimizing Store Listings: When publishing games on digital distribution platforms like Steam, itch.io, or the App Store, optimizing store listings is crucial for attracting players and improving discoverability. Pygame developers should craft compelling store descriptions, choose relevant keywords, and select appealing visuals to optimize their game's store page. By highlighting key features, gameplay mechanics, and unique selling points, developers can effectively communicate the value proposition of their game and convince players to explore further or make a purchase.

Building a Community and Engaging with Fans: Building a dedicated community of fans and supporters is essential for long-term success and sustainability. Pygame developers can create Discord servers, Reddit communities, or official forums where players can discuss the game, share fan art, and provide feedback. By actively engaging with fans, responding to questions, and involving them in the development process, developers can foster a sense of ownership and loyalty among their community members, turning them into ambassadors who advocate for the game and help spread the word organically.

Launching Promotions and Sales: Running promotions, discounts, and sales can help boost visibility, drive traffic, and increase sales for games on digital distribution platforms. Pygame developers can strategically plan and execute limited-time discounts, seasonal sales, or bundle deals to attract attention and incentivize players to purchase their games. Additionally, participating in platform-specific events like Steam's seasonal sales or itch.io's bundle promotions can provide developers with additional exposure and opportunities to reach new audiences.

Seeking Press Coverage and Reviews: Securing press coverage and reviews from gaming journalists, bloggers, and YouTubers can significantly raise awareness and credibility for a game. Pygame developers should prepare press kits containing press releases, review copies, screenshots, and trailers to distribute to relevant media outlets and influencers. By pitching their game to gaming publications, podcasts, and YouTube channels, developers can increase the chances of getting coverage and reviews that can reach a broader audience and influence players' purchasing decisions.

Post-release Support and Updates

ONCE A GAME IS RELEASED, the work of a developer is far from over. Post-release support and updates are essential for maintaining player engagement, addressing issues, and improving the overall experience of the game. In this section, we'll explore the importance of post-release support and discuss strategies for effectively managing updates and responding to player feedback.

Bug Fixes and Performance Optimization: After a game is released, developers should closely monitor player feedback and reports to identify and address any bugs, glitches, or performance issues that may arise. Promptly releasing patches and updates to fix critical issues not only improves the stability and reliability of the game but also demonstrates the developer's commitment to delivering a polished and enjoyable experience to players.

Adding New Content and Features: To keep players engaged and excited about the game, developers can release updates that introduce new content, features, or gameplay mechanics. This could include new levels, characters, weapons, modes, or customization options that expand the game's replay value and offer fresh experiences to players. By listening to player feedback and observing trends, developers can prioritize and implement features that align with the community's interests and preferences.

Community Engagement and Feedback: Maintaining open communication channels with the player community is crucial for fostering a positive relationship and gathering valuable feedback. Developers can actively engage with players through social media, forums, Discord servers, and live streams to solicit feedback, answer questions, and address concerns. By listening to player suggestions and incorporating community-driven ideas into updates, developers can make players feel valued and involved in the game's ongoing development.

Transparency and Roadmaps: Providing transparency about the development roadmap and upcoming updates can help manage player expectations and build anticipation for future content releases. Developers can share detailed roadmaps outlining planned features, improvements, and timelines for upcoming updates, allowing players to know what to expect and when to expect it. By regularly updating the community on progress and milestones, developers can instill confidence and trust in their ability to deliver on their promises.

Balancing and Tuning: Achieving a balanced and enjoyable gameplay experience requires ongoing tuning and iteration based on player data and feedback. Developers should closely monitor gameplay metrics, such as win rates, player progression, and engagement metrics, to identify areas that may require balancing adjustments. By carefully tweaking game mechanics, difficulty levels, and progression systems, developers can ensure that the game remains fair, challenging, and rewarding for players of all skill levels.

Localization and Accessibility: Expanding accessibility and reaching new markets can significantly broaden the game's audience and increase its overall impact. Developers can prioritize localization efforts to translate the game into different languages and tailor the experience to suit the cultural preferences and sensitivities of diverse player demographics. Additionally, implementing accessibility features such as customizable controls, subtitles, colorblind modes, and adjustable difficulty settings can make the game more inclusive and enjoyable for players with disabilities or special needs.

Promotional Events and Community Challenges: Hosting promotional events, contests, and community challenges can inject excitement and engagement into the game's community. Developers can organize themed events, tournaments, or in-game challenges that encourage players to compete, collaborate, and showcase their skills. By offering exclusive rewards, prizes, or recognition for participants, developers can incentivize player participation and create memorable experiences that strengthen community bonds and increase player retention.

Long-term Support and Sustainability: Supporting a game over the long term requires careful planning, resource allocation, and commitment from developers. Even after the initial launch hype subsides, developers should continue to release periodic updates, patches, and content expansions to keep the game relevant and maintain player interest. By cultivating a dedicated player community, establishing sustainable revenue streams, and fostering a culture of continuous improvement, developers can ensure the long-term success and longevity of their game in a competitive market landscape.

Chapter 14: Advanced Graphics and Effects

Working with Advanced 2D Effects

IN THIS SECTION, WE'LL delve into the realm of advanced 2D effects in Pygame, exploring techniques to enhance the visual appeal and immersion of your games. By leveraging various graphical effects and rendering techniques, you can create stunning visuals that captivate players and elevate the overall aesthetic of your game.

Sprite Blending and Transparency: One of the fundamental techniques for creating visually appealing graphics is sprite blending and transparency. By adjusting the alpha channel of sprites, you can control their opacity and create smooth transitions between overlapping objects. This technique is particularly useful for implementing effects such as shadows, reflections, and translucent surfaces, adding depth and realism to your game's visuals.

Particle Systems: Particle systems are a powerful tool for simulating natural phenomena such as fire, smoke, water, and explosions. By emitting a large number of small, animated sprites called particles, you can create dynamic and immersive effects that enhance the atmosphere and excitement of your game. Pygame provides built-in support for implementing particle systems, making it easy to integrate complex visual effects into your game without the need for advanced graphics programming.

Shader Effects: Shaders are programs written in a specialized language such as GLSL (OpenGL Shading Language) that run directly on the GPU (Graphics Processing Unit). By applying shaders to sprites or the entire screen, you can achieve a wide range of visual effects, including dynamic lighting, post-processing effects, distortion effects, and more. Shaders allow for advanced manipulation of pixels and vertices, enabling you to create stunning visual effects that would be difficult or impossible to achieve with traditional rendering techniques.

Texture Mapping and UV Mapping: Texture mapping is a technique for applying images, called textures, to the surfaces of 3D objects to simulate complex surface details and patterns. In Pygame, you can use texture mapping to enhance the visual fidelity of sprites and environments by applying high-resolution textures with intricate designs and realistic textures. UV mapping is the process of mapping points on a 3D surface to coordinates in a 2D texture, allowing for precise control over how textures are applied and distorted on the surface of objects.

Advanced Animation Techniques: To bring your game to life, it's essential to employ advanced animation techniques that go beyond simple sprite sheet animations. Pygame provides support for skeletal animation, inverse kinematics, and procedural animation, allowing you to create fluid, natural-looking animations that respond dynamically to player input and environmental conditions. By combining these techniques with advanced graphics effects such as motion blur, depth of field, and chromatic aberration, you can create visually stunning animations that enhance the immersion and realism of your game.

Layering and Parallax Scrolling: Layering and parallax scrolling are techniques for creating the illusion of depth and perspective in 2D games by moving layers of sprites at different speeds relative to the camera. By separating the game world into multiple layers and scrolling them independently, you can simulate the effect of objects appearing closer or farther away, adding depth and dimensionality to the scene. Parallax scrolling is commonly used in side-scrolling and top-down games to create visually interesting backgrounds and foreground elements that enhance the sense of immersion and scale.

Dynamic Lighting and Shadows: Lighting and shadows play a crucial role in establishing the mood, atmosphere, and realism of a game environment. Pygame provides support for dynamic lighting and shadows through techniques such as shadow mapping, stencil shadows, and light attenuation. By simulating the interaction of light sources with objects in the game world, you can create dynamic, realistic lighting effects that dynamically change based on the position, intensity, and color of light sources. This adds depth, drama, and visual interest to your game's environments, making them more engaging and immersive for players.

Advanced Camera Effects: The camera is a powerful tool for controlling the player's view of the game world and directing their attention to important elements and events. Pygame allows you to implement advanced camera effects such as zooming, panning, and rotation, as well as effects like screen shake, motion blur, and depth of field. These effects can be used to create cinematic sequences, emphasize dramatic moments, or simulate the effects of a handheld camera, adding cinematic flair and dynamism to your game's visuals.

Implementing Particle Systems

PARTICLE SYSTEMS ARE a powerful tool for adding dynamic and immersive effects to your games. In this section, we'll explore how to implement particle systems in Pygame to create effects such as fire, smoke, explosions, and more.

Particle Generation: The first step in implementing a particle system is to generate particles at regular intervals or in response to specific events. Each particle is represented by a small, animated sprite that moves, changes size, and fades over time. You can control various parameters of the particles, such as their initial position, velocity, acceleration, lifespan, color, and transparency, to create a wide range of effects.

Particle Behavior: Once particles are generated, you need to define their behavior over time. This typically involves updating the position, velocity, and other attributes of each particle in each frame of the game loop. For example, you might simulate gravity by applying a downward acceleration to particles, or simulate wind by applying a lateral force. You can also introduce randomness to create more natural-looking effects, such as varying the speed and direction of particles or adding turbulence to their motion.

Collision Detection: In some cases, you may want particles to interact with other objects in the game world, such as walls, obstacles, or other particles. Implementing collision detection for particles can be challenging but rewarding, as it allows you to create more complex and realistic effects. You can use techniques such as bounding box collision detection or pixel-perfect collision detection to detect collisions between particles and other objects and respond accordingly, such as bouncing off walls or exploding on impact.

Particle Rendering: Once particles are generated and updated, you need to render them to the screen. Pygame provides built-in support for rendering sprites, making it easy to display particles as animated sprites on the screen. You can use techniques such as alpha blending and transparency to create smooth transitions between particles and blend them seamlessly with the background. You can also apply color gradients, texture mapping, and other visual effects to enhance the appearance of particles and make them more visually appealing.

Optimization: Particle systems can be computationally expensive, especially if you have a large number of particles or complex particle behavior. To ensure optimal performance, it's important to implement efficient algorithms and data structures for updating and rendering particles. For example, you can use spatial partitioning techniques such as quad trees or spatial hashing to quickly determine which particles are within the vicinity of other objects in the game world and need to be updated or rendered. You can also use techniques such as object pooling to reuse particle objects instead of creating and destroying them every frame, reducing memory allocation overhead.

Advanced Effects: Once you have a basic particle system up and running, you can experiment with advanced effects to create more visually stunning and immersive effects. For example, you can implement particle blending modes to create additive or subtractive blending effects, allowing particles to interact with each other and the background in interesting ways. You can also add trails, sparks, sparks, or other secondary effects to particles to enhance their appearance and create more dynamic and engaging effects.

Integration with Game Logic: Finally, it's important to integrate the particle system with the rest of your game logic to ensure that particles respond appropriately to game events and player actions.

For example, you might trigger a particle explosion when a bomb detonates or generate a burst of sparks when a character takes damage. By synchronizing particle effects with game events, you can create more immersive and responsive gameplay experiences that keep players engaged and entertained.

Utilizing Shaders for Visual Effects

SHADERS ARE POWERFUL tools for creating sophisticated visual effects in games. In this section, we'll explore how to utilize shaders in Pygame to enhance the graphics and create stunning visual effects.

What are Shaders?: Shaders are small programs written in a specialized shading language, such as GLSL (OpenGL Shading Language) or HLSL (High-Level Shading Language), that run directly on the GPU (Graphics Processing Unit). Shaders allow you to manipulate the appearance of objects and scenes in real-time by performing calculations for each pixel or vertex in the scene.

Types of Shaders: There are two main types of shaders: vertex shaders and fragment shaders. Vertex shaders operate on individual vertices of 3D models and are responsible for transforming vertices from object space to screen space. Fragment shaders, also known as pixel shaders, operate on individual pixels of the rendered image and are responsible for calculating the color of each pixel based on various factors such as lighting, texture mapping, and material properties.

Shader Programs: Shaders are typically organized into shader programs, which consist of one or more shader stages, such as vertex shaders, fragment shaders, and geometry shaders. Shader programs are compiled and linked together to form a complete rendering pipeline that processes vertices and pixels to produce the final rendered image.

Integration with Pygame: Pygame provides limited support for shaders out of the box, but you can still use shaders to create visual effects by leveraging third-party libraries such as Pygame-SGE

(Pygame Shader Graph Extension) or PyOpenGL. These libraries provide APIs for loading and compiling shaders, setting shader parameters, and applying shaders to sprites and surfaces in Pygame.

Common Visual Effects: With shaders, you can create a wide range of visual effects, including dynamic lighting, shadows, reflections, refractions, water simulations, particle effects, and more. For example, you can use shaders to simulate realistic lighting effects by implementing techniques such as Phong shading, Blinn-Phong shading, or physically-based rendering (PBR). You can also create procedural textures and apply them to objects using fragment shaders to add detail and variation to the scene.

Performance Considerations: While shaders can create stunning visual effects, they can also be computationally expensive, especially if you have complex shader programs or a large number of objects in the scene. To ensure optimal performance, it's important to carefully optimize your shaders and minimize unnecessary computations. You can use techniques such as shader caching, shader pre-compilation, and shader LOD (Level of Detail) to reduce shader compilation times and improve rendering performance.

Cross-Platform Compatibility: When using shaders in Pygame, it's important to consider cross-platform compatibility, as shaders may behave differently on different GPU architectures and driver versions. To ensure compatibility, it's recommended to test your shaders on a variety of hardware configurations and fallback to alternative rendering paths or techniques if necessary.

Shader Libraries and Resources: There are many resources available online for learning about shaders and finding shader code snippets and examples. Websites such as ShaderToy, Shadertoy.com, and The Book of Shaders provide a wealth of shader code samples and tutorials for creating various visual effects. Additionally, there are numerous shader libraries and frameworks available for Pygame and other game development platforms that provide pre-built shaders and tools for creating custom shaders.

Conclusion: Shaders are powerful tools for creating stunning visual effects in games. By leveraging shaders in Pygame, you can enhance the graphics of your games and create immersive and engaging experiences for players. Whether you're creating realistic lighting effects, dynamic particle systems, or procedural textures, shaders offer endless possibilities for creative expression and artistic experimentation.

Integrating 3D Elements in Pygame

INTEGRATING 3D ELEMENTS into Pygame can significantly enhance the visual quality and gameplay experience of your games. In this section, we'll explore various techniques and libraries for integrating 3D graphics into Pygame applications.

3D Rendering Engines: One approach to integrating 3D graphics into Pygame is to use a 3D rendering engine or library. Libraries such as Panda3D, PyOpenGL, and Pygame3D provide APIs for creating and rendering 3D models, applying textures and materials, and implementing lighting and shading effects. These libraries typically use OpenGL or DirectX under the hood to perform hardware-accelerated 3D rendering.

Loading 3D Models: To display 3D models in Pygame, you first need to load the models from external file formats such as OBJ, FBX, or COLLADA. Libraries like PyAssimp and PyWavefront provide APIs for loading 3D models from various file formats and converting them into a format that can be rendered by Pygame.

Rendering 3D Models: Once you've loaded a 3D model into Pygame, you can render it to the screen using a combination of transformation matrices, view matrices, and projection matrices. You can apply transformations such as translation, rotation, and scaling to position and orient the model in 3D space, and then use perspective or orthographic projection to project the 3D scene onto a 2D viewport.

Camera and View Controls: Implementing camera controls is essential for navigating and exploring 3D environments in Pygame. You can implement basic camera controls such as pan, tilt, and zoom using keyboard or mouse input, or you can create more advanced camera systems with features like first-person or third-person perspectives, free-look camera, and orbit camera.

Implementing Lighting and Shading: Lighting and shading are crucial for creating realistic 3D graphics in Pygame. You can implement various lighting models such as ambient, diffuse, specular, and emissive lighting using shaders and materials. Shading techniques such as Phong shading, Blinn-Phong shading, and physically-based rendering (PBR) can enhance the visual quality of your 3D scenes and make them more immersive and engaging.

Optimizing 3D Performance: Rendering complex 3D scenes in Pygame can be computationally intensive, especially on lower-end hardware. To ensure optimal performance, it's important to optimize your 3D rendering code and minimize unnecessary computations. You can use techniques such as frustum culling, occlusion culling, level of detail (LOD), and batching to reduce the number of draw calls and improve rendering performance.

Cross-Platform Compatibility: When integrating 3D graphics into Pygame, it's important to consider cross-platform compatibility, as 3D rendering behavior may vary across different operating systems and GPU architectures. To ensure compatibility, it's recommended to test your 3D rendering code on a variety of hardware configurations and fallback to alternative rendering paths or techniques if necessary.

Conclusion: Integrating 3D elements into Pygame can take your games to the next level by adding depth, realism, and interactivity to the visual experience. Whether you're creating immersive 3D environments, realistic character models, or dynamic special effects, the techniques and libraries discussed in this section provide a solid foundation for building compelling 3D games in Pygame. With the right tools and techniques, you can unleash your creativity and bring your game ideas to life in stunning 3D detail.

Creating Dynamic Lighting and Shadows

DYNAMIC LIGHTING AND shadows add depth and realism to game environments, enhancing the visual appeal and immersiveness of gameplay. In this section, we'll explore techniques for implementing dynamic lighting and shadows in Pygame.

Light Sources: The first step in implementing dynamic lighting is to define light sources within your game world. Light sources can include point lights, directional lights, spotlights, and ambient lights. Each light source emits light rays that interact with objects in the scene, illuminating surfaces and casting shadows.

Lighting Models: There are various lighting models you can use to simulate the interaction between light sources and surfaces in your game world. Common lighting models include Lambertian diffuse reflection, Blinn-Phong specular reflection, and physically-based rendering (PBR). These models calculate the intensity and color of light reflected off surfaces based on their material properties and the angle of incidence.

Shadow Mapping: Shadow mapping is a popular technique for generating dynamic shadows in 3D graphics. It works by rendering the scene from the perspective of the light source and recording depth values (or depth maps) of visible surfaces from the light's point of view. These depth maps are then used to determine which areas of the scene are in shadow and which are illuminated, allowing you to cast realistic shadows onto surfaces.

Shadow Projection: Once you have generated depth maps from the light's perspective, you can project these shadow maps onto the surfaces of objects in the scene. By comparing the depth values stored in the shadow maps with the depth values of pixels in the scene, you can determine whether a pixel is in shadow or not. Pixels that are occluded by objects in the scene will be shaded darker, creating the illusion of shadows.

Soft Shadows: In addition to hard shadows, you can also simulate soft shadows by applying a blur or falloff effect to the shadow maps. Soft shadows occur when light rays are partially blocked by translucent or semi-transparent objects, resulting in gradual transitions between light and shadow. By blurring the edges of shadows, you can create more realistic lighting effects and enhance the visual quality of your game scenes.

Performance Considerations: Generating dynamic lighting and shadows can be computationally intensive, especially in real-time applications like games. To optimize performance, you can use techniques such as light culling, shadow map caching, and level-of-detail (LOD) rendering to reduce the number of calculations and minimize rendering overhead. Additionally, you can experiment with rendering techniques like deferred shading or forward rendering to achieve better performance in complex scenes.

Artistic Considerations: When implementing dynamic lighting and shadows, it's important to consider the artistic style and mood of your game. The choice of lighting colors, intensity, and direction can have a significant impact on the atmosphere and tone of your game world. Experiment with different lighting setups and shadow effects to achieve the desired aesthetic and create memorable visual experiences for players.

Conclusion: Dynamic lighting and shadows are powerful tools for enhancing the visual quality and realism of your games. By carefully implementing lighting models, shadow mapping techniques, and performance optimizations, you can create immersive and visually stunning game environments that captivate players and bring your game worlds to life. Experiment with different lighting setups and shadow effects to find the perfect balance between realism and performance in your Pygame projects.

Leveraging External Libraries

Integrating Pygame with Other Python Libraries

INTEGRATING PYGAME with other Python libraries can greatly expand the capabilities and features of your game projects. Python has a rich ecosystem of libraries for various purposes, including graphics, physics simulation, artificial intelligence, networking, and more. In this section, we'll explore some of the most popular external libraries that can be used in conjunction with Pygame to enhance your games.

PyOpenGL: PyOpenGL is a Python binding for the OpenGL graphics library, which is widely used for rendering 2D and 3D graphics in computer games and simulations. By integrating Pygame with PyOpenGL, you can leverage OpenGL's powerful rendering capabilities to create visually stunning graphics and special effects in your games. PyOpenGL provides Python bindings for OpenGL functions, allowing you to access low-level graphics programming features directly from your Pygame code.

Pygame_gui: Pygame_gui is a user interface library for Pygame that provides a set of GUI components and widgets for creating interactive user interfaces in Pygame applications. Pygame_gui allows you to easily design and implement menus, buttons, sliders, text boxes, and other UI elements in your games, without having to write low-level Pygame code. It provides a higher-level abstraction layer for managing GUI components, making it easier to create polished and professional-looking user interfaces in Pygame.

PyTMX: PyTMX is a Python library for loading and parsing Tiled Map Editor (Tiled) files, which are commonly used for designing tile-based game levels and maps. PyTMX allows you to import Tiled maps directly into your Pygame projects, making it easy to create complex and detailed game environments with minimal effort. It provides functions for loading tilesets, layers, objects, and properties from Tiled maps, allowing you to access and manipulate map data within your Pygame code.

Pygame_sdl2: Pygame_sdl2 is an alternative implementation of the Pygame library that uses the Simple DirectMedia Layer (SDL2) as its backend instead of the original SDL library. Pygame_sdl2 provides better performance and cross-platform compatibility compared to the original Pygame library, making it a popular choice for developing high-performance games with Pygame. It provides Python bindings for SDL2 functions, allowing you to access low-level multimedia and input/output features directly from your Pygame code.

Pygame_network: Pygame_network is a Python library for networking and multiplayer game development with Pygame. It provides functions for creating client-server architectures, sending and receiving network messages, synchronizing game states over a network, and handling multiplayer game sessions. Pygame_network simplifies the process of implementing networked multiplayer functionality in Pygame projects, allowing you to focus on gameplay mechanics and user experience.

Pygame_ml: Pygame_ml is a machine learning library for Pygame that provides functions for training and deploying machine learning models in Pygame applications. Pygame_ml allows you to integrate AI-driven gameplay mechanics, character behaviors, and decision-making processes into your games, using techniques such as reinforcement learning, neural networks, genetic algorithms, and more. It provides a set of pre-trained models and algorithms for common game AI tasks, as well as tools for training custom models on game data.

Conclusion: Integrating Pygame with external libraries can unlock a wealth of new possibilities and features for your game projects. Whether you're looking to add advanced graphics effects, create interactive user interfaces, design complex game levels, optimize performance, implement multiplayer functionality, or integrate AI-driven gameplay mechanics, there's a Python library out there to help you achieve your goals. Experiment with different libraries and techniques to find the perfect combination for your Pygame projects, and take your games to the next level.

Enhancing Pygame with OpenGL for 3D Graphics

PYGAME IS PRIMARILY known for 2D game development, but with the integration of OpenGL, you can add 3D graphics to your Pygame projects. OpenGL is a cross-platform API for rendering 2D and 3D graphics, providing low-level access to the GPU for high-performance rendering. By combining Pygame with OpenGL, you can create immersive 3D environments, realistic lighting effects, and dynamic visual effects in your games.

OpenGL operates on a state machine paradigm, where you set various rendering states and issue rendering commands to the GPU. Pygame provides a way to create an OpenGL context and interact with OpenGL functions using the pygame.GL module. You can initialize an OpenGL context using pygame.display.set_mode() with the pygame.OPENGL flag.

Once the OpenGL context is set up, you can start issuing OpenGL commands to render graphics. This includes setting up the projection matrix, defining vertex data, specifying shaders, and issuing rendering commands. Pygame provides functions like glBegin() and glEnd() for specifying geometric primitives, such as points, lines, and triangles. You can also use vertex buffer objects (VBOs) and vertex array objects (VAOs) for more efficient rendering.

To add textures to your 3D models, you can use the glTexImage2D() function to load images as textures and bind them to OpenGL texture units. You can then apply textures to your geometry using texture coordinates and texture mapping techniques. Pygame provides functions like pygame.image.load() to load image files, which can be converted to texture data using the pygame.image.tostring() function.

Shaders are essential for implementing advanced graphics effects in OpenGL. Shaders are small programs that run on the GPU and control various aspects of the rendering pipeline, such as vertex transformations, lighting calculations, and fragment coloring. Pygame allows you to load and compile shader programs using the OpenGL.GL.shaders module, and attach them to your rendering pipeline using the glUseProgram() function.

In addition to rendering 3D models, you can also implement advanced lighting effects using OpenGL. This includes techniques such as per-pixel lighting, ambient occlusion, shadow mapping, and specular highlights. Pygame provides functions for setting up lights, materials, and other lighting parameters, allowing you to create realistic lighting effects in your 3D scenes.

When working with OpenGL in Pygame, it's essential to understand the underlying OpenGL concepts and techniques, such as coordinate transformations, projection matrices, vertex and fragment shaders, and rendering optimizations. By mastering these concepts, you can unleash the full potential of OpenGL and create visually stunning 3D graphics in your Pygame projects.

Overall, integrating Pygame with OpenGL opens up a world of possibilities for creating immersive 3D games and simulations. Whether you're building a first-person shooter, a racing game, or a virtual reality experience, OpenGL provides the tools and techniques you need to bring your ideas to life in stunning detail and realism. Experiment with different OpenGL features and techniques to create unique visual effects and push the boundaries of what's possible in Pygame game development.

Using AI and Machine Learning Libraries

PYGAME CAN BE ENHANCED with the integration of various AI and machine learning libraries, enabling advanced gameplay mechanics, intelligent opponents, and adaptive game environments. These libraries provide powerful tools and algorithms for implementing artificial intelligence (AI) behaviors, training models, and analyzing game data. By leveraging these libraries, you can create more engaging and immersive gaming experiences in Pygame.

One popular AI and machine learning library for Python is TensorFlow. TensorFlow is an open-source platform for machine learning and deep learning, developed by Google. It provides a comprehensive ecosystem of tools and libraries for building and deploying machine learning models, including neural networks, reinforcement learning algorithms, and natural language processing (NLP) models. With TensorFlow, you can train AI models to recognize patterns, make predictions, and learn from game data to improve gameplay.

Another widely used library is PyTorch, developed by Facebook. PyTorch is a deep learning framework that offers dynamic computational graphs and a flexible programming interface, making it ideal for research and development in AI and machine learning. PyTorch provides modules for building neural networks, training models, and optimizing performance, allowing you to implement complex AI behaviors and strategies in your Pygame projects.

For reinforcement learning tasks, you can use libraries like OpenAI Gym and Stable Baselines. OpenAI Gym is a toolkit for developing and comparing reinforcement learning algorithms, providing a collection of environments for training and testing AI agents. Stable Baselines is a set of high-quality implementations of reinforcement learning algorithms, built on top of OpenAI Gym, making it easy to train AI agents for various tasks, such as game playing, robotic control, and optimization.

In addition to deep learning and reinforcement learning, you can also use libraries for other AI techniques, such as genetic algorithms, fuzzy logic, and decision trees. These libraries offer alternative approaches to AI programming and can be useful for implementing specific behaviors or solving particular problems in your games.

When integrating AI and machine learning libraries with Pygame, it's essential to understand the principles and techniques behind these algorithms and how they can be applied to game development. This includes concepts such as supervised learning, unsupervised learning, reinforcement learning, model training, and evaluation metrics. By mastering these concepts, you can design AI systems that enhance gameplay, challenge players, and adapt to changing game conditions dynamically.

Overall, integrating AI and machine learning libraries with Pygame opens up new possibilities for game design and development. Whether you're creating intelligent opponents, adaptive game environments, or procedural content generation systems, AI and machine learning can take your Pygame projects to the next level. Experiment with different libraries and techniques to discover innovative ways to enhance your games and engage your players.

Networking Enhancements with External Modules

NETWORKING IS ESSENTIAL for developing multiplayer games, online leaderboards, and real-time communication between players. Pygame can be extended with external modules to facilitate networking functionalities, allowing developers to create connected gaming experiences and multiplayer interactions.

One popular networking library for Python is socket. The socket module provides low-level networking primitives for creating sockets, sending and receiving data over TCP/IP or UDP, and establishing connections between clients and servers. With socket, you can implement custom networking protocols, handle network events, and synchronize game states across multiple clients.

Another option is to use higher-level networking frameworks like Twisted or asyncio. Twisted is an event-driven networking engine that supports various protocols and transports, making it suitable for building scalable and robust networked applications. asyncio, on the other hand, is a standard library module for asynchronous I/O operations, allowing you to write concurrent networking code with coroutines and event loops.

For real-time communication and multiplayer gaming, you can leverage dedicated networking libraries such as PodSixNet and pygame-network. PodSixNet is a lightweight networking library specifically designed for game development, providing easy-to-use APIs for creating multiplayer games with client-server architecture. pygame-network, on the other hand, is a networking extension for Pygame that simplifies the process of building networked games by handling low-level networking details and providing high-level abstractions for sending and receiving game data.

Additionally, cloud-based networking solutions like Google Cloud and AWS (Amazon Web Services) offer scalable and reliable infrastructure for hosting multiplayer game servers, managing player sessions, and handling network traffic. These platforms provide various services, including virtual machines, databases, load balancers, and content delivery networks (CDNs), to support online multiplayer games with global reach and high availability.

When integrating networking enhancements with Pygame, it's essential to consider factors like latency, bandwidth, security, and scalability. By optimizing network performance, implementing efficient data synchronization mechanisms, and designing robust network architectures, you can ensure smooth and responsive multiplayer experiences for players.

In summary, external networking modules and libraries enable developers to extend Pygame's networking capabilities and create connected gaming experiences. Whether you're building real-time multiplayer games, online leaderboards, or social features, leveraging these tools can help you deliver engaging and interactive gameplay experiences that keep players coming back for more. Experiment with different networking frameworks and platforms to find the best solution for your game's networking needs.

Exploring Libraries for Advanced Game Features

AS GAME DEVELOPMENT continues to evolve, developers seek to implement increasingly sophisticated features to enhance gameplay and create immersive experiences for players. Fortunately, the Python ecosystem offers a wide range of libraries and tools that complement Pygame's capabilities and enable the implementation of advanced game features.

One such library is PyOpenGL, which provides bindings for OpenGL (Open Graphics Library), a powerful cross-platform API for rendering 2D and 3D graphics. By integrating PyOpenGL with Pygame, developers can leverage hardware-accelerated rendering, shader programming, and advanced graphics techniques to create visually stunning games with smooth animations, realistic effects, and immersive environments.

Another essential tool for advanced game development is NumPy, a powerful library for numerical computing in Python. NumPy's multidimensional array objects and mathematical functions enable efficient data manipulation, collision detection, physics simulation, and procedural content generation in Pygame. By leveraging NumPy's capabilities, developers can optimize game performance, implement complex algorithms, and handle large datasets with ease.

For AI and machine learning-driven gameplay, developers can explore libraries like TensorFlow and PyTorch. These deep learning frameworks provide tools for training and deploying neural networks, enabling intelligent behavior, adaptive gameplay, and procedural content generation in Pygame. With TensorFlow and PyTorch, developers can create AI-driven NPCs, generate dynamic game levels, and personalize player experiences based on real-time data and feedback.

In addition to graphics and AI, audio is another crucial aspect of game development. Libraries like PyDub and LibROSA offer tools for audio processing, manipulation, and analysis, allowing developers to create immersive soundscapes, interactive music systems, and dynamic audio effects in Pygame. By integrating audio libraries with Pygame, developers can enhance gameplay immersion, evoke emotions, and create memorable audio experiences for players.

Furthermore, for advanced physics simulation and game dynamics, developers can explore libraries like Box2D and PyODE. These physics engines provide realistic collision detection, rigid body dynamics, and fluid simulation capabilities, enabling developers to create physics-based puzzles, vehicle simulations, and interactive environments in Pygame. By integrating physics engines with Pygame, developers can add depth and realism to their games, enhancing player engagement and immersion.

Lastly, for networking and multiplayer features, developers can leverage libraries like WebSocket and Socket.IO. These libraries provide tools for real-time communication, multiplayer synchronization, and server-client interaction, enabling developers to create connected gaming experiences and online multiplayer games with Pygame. By implementing networking features, developers can expand their game's reach, foster community engagement, and provide social experiences for players.

In conclusion, the Python ecosystem offers a rich variety of libraries and tools for enhancing Pygame with advanced game features. By exploring these libraries and leveraging their capabilities, developers can push the boundaries of game development, create immersive experiences, and captivate players with innovative gameplay mechanics, stunning visuals, and dynamic audio. Experimenting with different libraries and integrating them into Pygame projects opens up new possibilities for creativity and innovation in game design and development.

Chapter 16: Game Design Principles

Understanding Game Mechanics and Dynamics

GAME MECHANICS AND dynamics form the backbone of any video game, defining how players interact with the game world and each other. Mechanics refer to the rules and systems governing gameplay, while dynamics describe the emergent behaviors and experiences that arise from those mechanics. Understanding these elements is crucial for game designers seeking to create engaging and immersive experiences.

At its core, game design revolves around the interplay between mechanics and dynamics. Mechanics provide the framework within which players operate, dictating the available actions, objectives, and constraints. These can range from simple movement controls in platformers to complex combat systems in role-playing games. Mechanics establish the rules of the game, defining what is and isn't possible within its virtual world.

However, it's the dynamics that truly bring a game to life. Dynamics emerge from the interaction between players and mechanics, resulting in the varied experiences and outcomes that define gameplay. For example, in a multiplayer shooter, the dynamic interactions between players, weapons, and level layouts create tense firefights, stealthy maneuvers, and strategic team play.

One of the key challenges in game design is crafting mechanics that give rise to compelling dynamics. This requires a deep understanding of player motivations, preferences, and behaviors. By aligning mechanics with player desires, designers can create experiences that are not only enjoyable but also meaningful and memorable.

Effective game mechanics are intuitive, easy to learn, and hard to master. They provide players with a clear set of rules and objectives while allowing for creative expression and strategic decision-making. Whether it's jumping over obstacles in a platformer or managing resources in a strategy game, mechanics should offer a satisfying balance of challenge and reward.

In addition to creating engaging gameplay, game mechanics can also serve as powerful storytelling tools. By integrating narrative elements into gameplay systems, designers can immerse players in rich, interactive worlds where their actions have real consequences. For example, moral choices in role-playing games or branching dialogue options in narrative-driven adventures can shape the outcome of the story and the player's journey.

Another aspect of game design is balancing complexity and accessibility. While deep and intricate mechanics can provide depth and longevity to a game, they also run the risk of alienating casual players. Striking the right balance between depth and accessibility is crucial for ensuring that a game appeals to a broad audience while still offering depth for experienced players to explore.

Iterative design and playtesting are essential components of the game design process, allowing designers to refine and improve mechanics based on player feedback and data. By observing how players interact with the game and analyzing their behavior, designers can identify areas for improvement and make informed decisions about which mechanics to tweak, expand, or remove altogether.

Ultimately, successful game design requires a holistic approach that considers the interplay between mechanics, dynamics, and player experience. By creating compelling mechanics that give rise to engaging dynamics, designers can craft immersive and memorable gaming experiences that resonate with players long after they've put down the controller.

Crafting Engaging Game Narratives

CRAFTING AN ENGAGING game narrative is a complex and multifaceted process that involves weaving together storytelling elements, player agency, and interactivity to create a compelling experience. Unlike traditional forms of narrative media like books or movies, game narratives must account for player choice and agency, allowing players to shape the story through their actions and decisions.

One of the key challenges in game narrative design is balancing player agency with authored storytelling. While linear narratives provide a structured and cohesive experience, they can limit player freedom and agency. On the other hand, open-ended narratives offer players more freedom to explore and shape the story, but they can also result in fragmented or disjointed experiences.

To strike the right balance, game designers often employ techniques such as branching dialogue trees, moral choices, and multiple endings to give players a sense of agency while still guiding them through a cohesive narrative arc. By providing meaningful choices and consequences, designers can create narratives that feel dynamic and responsive to player actions.

Another important aspect of game narrative design is world-building. Creating a rich and immersive game world helps to establish the setting, atmosphere, and tone of the narrative, drawing players into the game's universe and making them feel invested in the story. This can involve developing detailed lore, crafting believable characters, and designing visually striking environments that evoke a sense of wonder and discovery.

In addition to traditional storytelling techniques, game narratives can also leverage interactive elements such as environmental storytelling, emergent narratives, and player-driven storytelling. Environmental storytelling involves using environmental cues, props, and level design to convey narrative information without relying on explicit exposition. Emergent narratives arise from the dynamic interactions between players, NPCs, and game systems, resulting in unique and unpredictable storytelling experiences. Player-driven storytelling allows players to create their own narratives through their actions and interactions with the game world, fostering a sense of ownership and agency.

Collaboration between writers, designers, artists, and programmers is essential for creating cohesive and immersive game narratives. By working together to integrate narrative elements with gameplay systems and mechanics, teams can create seamless and immersive storytelling experiences that resonate with players on an emotional and intellectual level.

Iterative design and playtesting are crucial for refining and polishing game narratives. By gathering feedback from players and analyzing their responses, designers can identify areas for improvement and fine-tune the narrative to better resonate with the intended audience. This iterative process allows designers to craft narratives that are not only engaging and immersive but also emotionally resonant and thematically rich.

Overall, crafting engaging game narratives requires a combination of storytelling skill, creative vision, and technical expertise. By leveraging the unique strengths of the medium and embracing player agency and interactivity, designers can create narratives that captivate and inspire players, leaving a lasting impression long after the game is over.

Designing for Accessibility

DESIGNING GAMES WITH accessibility in mind is essential for ensuring that players of all abilities can enjoy and engage with the experience. Accessibility in gaming encompasses a wide range of considerations, including visual, auditory, motor, and cognitive accessibility.

Visual accessibility involves designing games that are easy to see and understand for players with visual impairments or disabilities. This can include features such as customizable text sizes and colors, high-contrast modes, and alternative visual cues for important gameplay information. Providing multiple options for displaying information can accommodate players with different visual preferences and needs.

Auditory accessibility focuses on making games accessible to players who are deaf or hard of hearing. This can involve providing subtitles or captions for dialogue and audio cues, as well as visual indicators for important sound effects or events. Additionally, providing alternative methods for conveying information, such as visual or tactile feedback, can help ensure that all players can fully experience the game.

Motor accessibility addresses the needs of players with mobility impairments or disabilities. Designing games with customizable controls, adjustable input sensitivity, and support for alternative input devices can make games more accessible to players with diverse motor abilities. Providing options for remapping controls and adjusting input settings can empower players to play the game in a way that is comfortable and accessible for them.

Cognitive accessibility focuses on making games understandable and enjoyable for players with cognitive impairments or disabilities. This can include features such as clear and concise instructions, intuitive user interfaces, and adjustable difficulty settings. Providing tutorials, hints, and in-game assistance can help players understand game mechanics and progress through the game at their own pace.

In addition to these specific considerations, designing games with accessibility in mind also involves adopting inclusive design principles that prioritize the needs and experiences of all players. This can include involving players with disabilities in the design and development process, conducting accessibility testing and feedback sessions, and actively seeking out and addressing barriers to accessibility.

By designing games with accessibility in mind from the outset, developers can create more inclusive and welcoming experiences for players of all abilities. By considering the diverse needs and preferences of players, developers can ensure that everyone can enjoy and engage with their games, regardless of their physical or cognitive abilities. Ultimately, accessible design benefits not only players with disabilities but the entire gaming community, making games more enjoyable and accessible for everyone.

Playtesting and User Feedback

PLAYTESTING AND GATHERING user feedback are crucial steps in the game development process. They provide valuable insights into how players interact with the game, identify areas for improvement, and help ensure that the final product meets players' expectations. In this section, we'll explore the importance of playtesting and user feedback and discuss strategies for effectively incorporating them into the development process.

One of the primary goals of playtesting is to identify any issues or bugs in the game that may impact the player experience. This can include technical issues such as crashes or glitches, as well as gameplay issues such as confusing mechanics or unbalanced difficulty. By observing players as they play the game and collecting feedback on their experiences, developers can identify these issues early in the development process and address them before release.

In addition to identifying technical and gameplay issues, playtesting also provides valuable insights into how players perceive and interact with the game. This can include feedback on the game's controls, interface design, level design, narrative, and overall enjoyment. By gathering feedback from a diverse group of players, developers can gain a better understanding of the game's strengths and weaknesses and make informed decisions about how to improve it.

There are several different approaches to playtesting, ranging from informal playtesting sessions with friends and family to more structured playtesting sessions with targeted groups of players. Informal playtesting sessions can provide valuable feedback on the game's core mechanics and overall fun factor, while structured playtesting sessions can provide more detailed feedback on specific aspects of the game.

User feedback can be gathered through a variety of methods, including surveys, interviews, focus groups, and online forums. Surveys and interviews allow developers to gather feedback from a large number of players in a relatively short amount of time, while focus groups and online forums allow for more in-depth discussions and interactions with players.

It's important for developers to listen carefully to user feedback and take it seriously, even if it contradicts their own opinions or expectations. Players are the ultimate judges of the game, and their feedback can provide valuable insights into how to improve it. Developers should be open to criticism and willing to make changes based on user feedback, even if it means rethinking or redesigning certain aspects of the game.

Iterative design is an important aspect of the playtesting process, as it allows developers to incorporate feedback and make improvements to the game over time. By continuously playtesting and gathering feedback throughout the development process, developers can ensure that the final product meets players' expectations and delivers a satisfying gaming experience.

In summary, playtesting and gathering user feedback are essential steps in the game development process. They provide valuable insights into how players interact with the game, identify areas for improvement, and help ensure that the final product meets players' expectations. By incorporating playtesting and user feedback into the development process, developers can create games that are enjoyable, engaging, and satisfying for players of all abilities.

The Art of Game Balancing

GAME BALANCING IS THE process of adjusting various game elements to ensure that the gameplay experience is fair, enjoyable, and challenging for players. It involves fine-tuning factors such as difficulty level, character abilities, enemy strength, resource availability, and more to create a balanced and engaging experience. In this section, we'll explore the art of game balancing and discuss strategies for achieving balance in different types of games.

One of the key goals of game balancing is to create a sense of challenge and progression for players. This often involves adjusting the difficulty curve to ensure that the game starts off relatively easy and gradually becomes more challenging as players progress. Balancing difficulty is a delicate process, as developers must strike a balance between providing a sufficient challenge to keep players engaged and preventing frustration from overly difficult sections.

Character abilities and enemy strength are also important factors to consider when balancing a game. Characters should feel powerful and capable, but not so overpowered that the game becomes too easy. Likewise, enemies should provide a reasonable challenge without being overwhelmingly difficult to defeat. Balancing character abilities and enemy strength requires careful consideration of factors such as damage output, health points, attack speed, and more.

Resource management is another aspect of game balancing that can significantly impact gameplay. Resources such as health potions, ammunition, and currency should be carefully distributed throughout the game to ensure that players have enough to progress without making the game too easy. Balancing resource availability requires careful consideration of factors such as resource scarcity, player skill level, and the overall pace of the game.

In multiplayer games, balancing is particularly important to ensure that all players have a fair and enjoyable experience. This often involves adjusting factors such as character abilities, weapon strengths, and map layouts to prevent any one player or team from having an unfair advantage. Balancing multiplayer games requires careful testing and iteration to identify and address any imbalances that may arise.

Iterative design is key to successful game balancing, as it allows developers to continuously test and adjust the game to achieve the desired balance. This may involve conducting playtests with real players, analyzing gameplay data, and making adjustments based on feedback and observations. By iterating on the game design and balance over time, developers can create a more polished and enjoyable experience for players.

In summary, game balancing is a critical aspect of game design that involves adjusting various game elements to ensure that the gameplay experience is fair, enjoyable, and challenging for players. Balancing difficulty, character abilities, enemy strength, resource availability, and other factors requires careful consideration and iteration to achieve the desired balance. By employing strategies such as iterative design and player feedback, developers can create games that are engaging, satisfying, and fun to play.

Chapter 17: Mobile Game Development with Pygame

Adapting Pygame Games for Mobile

MOBILE GAME DEVELOPMENT has become increasingly popular due to the widespread use of smartphones and tablets. With Pygame, developers can create games that run on mobile devices with some adaptation. Adapting Pygame games for mobile involves several considerations, including screen size, touch input, performance optimization, and distribution. In this section, we'll explore the process of adapting Pygame games for mobile platforms.

Screen size is a critical factor to consider when adapting Pygame games for mobile devices. Unlike desktop computers, mobile devices come in a variety of screen sizes and resolutions, ranging from small smartphones to large tablets. Developers must ensure that their games can adapt to different screen sizes without sacrificing gameplay or visual quality. This may involve implementing responsive design techniques or creating multiple versions of game assets optimized for different screen sizes.

Touch input is another key consideration for mobile game development. Unlike desktop games, which primarily rely on keyboard and mouse input, mobile games are typically controlled using touch gestures such as taps, swipes, and multi-touch gestures. Developers must design their games with touch input in mind, ensuring that controls are intuitive and responsive on touchscreen devices. This may involve redesigning user interfaces, implementing virtual joysticks or buttons, or optimizing touch sensitivity for precise input.

Performance optimization is essential for ensuring that Pygame games run smoothly on mobile devices. Mobile devices often have less processing power and memory than desktop computers, so developers must optimize their games to run efficiently on these platforms. This may involve optimizing game code, reducing the number of draw calls, minimizing texture memory usage, and implementing techniques such as object pooling and batch rendering to improve performance.

Distribution is the final step in adapting Pygame games for mobile platforms. Developers can distribute their games on mobile app stores such as the Apple App Store and Google Play Store, reaching millions of potential players worldwide. However, before releasing their games, developers must ensure that they meet the store's guidelines and requirements, including compatibility with different devices, adherence to platform-specific policies, and implementation of features such as in-app purchases and advertisements.

Overall, adapting Pygame games for mobile platforms involves several considerations, including screen size, touch input, performance optimization, and distribution. By carefully addressing these factors, developers can create mobile games that offer a seamless and enjoyable experience for players on smartphones and tablets. With the popularity of mobile gaming continuing to rise, adapting Pygame games for mobile platforms presents exciting opportunities for developers to reach a broad audience and create engaging gaming experiences.

Touch Input and Mobile Interface Design

WHEN DEVELOPING GAMES for mobile platforms using Pygame, touch input plays a crucial role in the overall user experience. Unlike traditional input methods like keyboards and mice, touchscreens offer a more intuitive and tactile interaction with games. In this section, we'll explore how to implement touch input in Pygame and discuss best practices for designing mobile interfaces.

Handling Touch Events

PYGAME PROVIDES SUPPORT for handling touch events through its event system. Touch events are similar to mouse events but are triggered by interactions with the touchscreen. Developers can listen for touch events using the pygame.event.get() function and then process them accordingly. For example, detecting a touch or swipe gesture can be done by checking for specific event types such as pygame.MOUSEBUTTONDOWN and pygame.MOUSEMOTION.

Multi-touch Gestures

MODERN MOBILE DEVICES support multi-touch gestures, allowing users to interact with the screen using multiple fingers simultaneously. Pygame provides built-in support for multi-touch input, making it possible to detect and process gestures like pinch-to-zoom, rotate, and multi-finger taps. Developers can utilize the pygame.touch.get_num_touches() function to determine the number of active touch points and pygame.touch.get_pos() to retrieve the positions of individual touch points.

Designing Mobile Interfaces

DESIGNING USER INTERFACES (UIs) for mobile games requires careful consideration of screen size, layout, and usability. Mobile interfaces should be optimized for touch input and provide clear visual feedback to users. Here are some best practices for designing mobile interfaces with Pygame:

1. **Responsive Layouts**: Design UI layouts that adapt to different screen sizes and orientations. Use relative positioning and flexible layouts to ensure that UI elements scale appropriately on various devices.

2. **Large Touch Targets**: Make interactive elements such as buttons and menus large enough to be easily tapped with a finger. Avoid placing interactive elements too close together to prevent accidental touches.

3. **Gestural Feedback**: Provide visual feedback for touch gestures to indicate to users that their actions have been recognized. This could include animations, color changes, or sound effects triggered by touch events.

4. **Consistent Navigation**: Maintain consistency in UI navigation patterns to help users navigate through different screens and menus seamlessly. Use familiar icons and gestures to minimize learning curves.

5. **Accessibility**: Ensure that your mobile interface is accessible to all users, including those with disabilities. Provide options for adjusting text size, color contrast, and other accessibility features.

Example Implementation

IMPORT pygame

import sys

```python
# Initialize Pygame
pygame.init()
# Set screen dimensions
screen_width = 800
screen_height = 600
screen = pygame.display.set_mode((screen_width, screen_height))
pygame.display.set_caption("Mobile Interface Example")
# Main game loop
running = True
while running:
    for event in pygame.event.get():
        if event.type == pygame.QUIT:
            running = False
        elif event.type == pygame.MOUSEBUTTONDOWN:
            # Handle touch input
            touch_pos = pygame.mouse.get_pos()
            print("Touch event at:", touch_pos)
    # Update display
    pygame.display.flip()
# Quit Pygame
```

pygame.quit()

sys.exit()

In this example, we create a simple Pygame window and listen for mouse/touch events. When a touch event occurs, the position of the touch is printed to the console. This demonstrates how to handle touch input in a Pygame application for mobile devices.

Conclusion

IMPLEMENTING TOUCH input and designing mobile interfaces are essential aspects of mobile game development with Pygame. By understanding how to handle touch events and following best practices for UI design, developers can create engaging and user-friendly mobile games that provide an immersive experience for players on smartphones and tablets.

Managing Resources on Mobile Devices

WHEN DEVELOPING GAMES for mobile platforms with Pygame, managing resources efficiently becomes crucial due to the limited memory and processing power of mobile devices compared to desktop computers. In this section, we'll discuss strategies for optimizing resource usage and maximizing performance on mobile devices.

Texture Compression

ONE COMMON TECHNIQUE for optimizing graphics performance on mobile devices is texture compression. By compressing textures, developers can reduce memory usage and improve rendering performance without sacrificing visual quality. Pygame supports various texture compression formats, such as ETC1 and PVRTC, which can be used to compress image assets before loading them into the game.

Asset Bundling

ANOTHER APPROACH TO resource management on mobile devices is asset bundling. Instead of loading individual assets separately, developers can bundle related assets into larger packages or archives. This reduces the number of file accesses and improves loading times, especially on devices with slower storage. Pygame provides tools for creating and loading asset bundles efficiently.

Memory Management

PROPER MEMORY MANAGEMENT is essential for preventing memory leaks and optimizing performance on mobile devices. Developers should be mindful of memory usage and release resources when they are no longer needed. Pygame offers functions for loading and unloading resources dynamically, allowing developers to manage memory more effectively during runtime.

Streaming Assets

FOR LARGE ASSETS SUCH as audio and video files, streaming can be a viable option to reduce memory usage and improve loading times. Instead of loading the entire asset into memory at once, developers can stream the data from disk or network as needed. Pygame provides support for streaming audio and video assets, allowing developers to play media files directly from external sources.

Asset Caching

CACHING FREQUENTLY used assets in memory can also help improve performance on mobile devices. By keeping frequently accessed resources in memory, developers can reduce loading times and avoid redundant disk access. Pygame provides mechanisms for caching assets, such as textures, sounds, and fonts, to optimize resource usage and enhance overall performance.

Example Implementation

IMPORT pygame

import os

 # Initialize Pygame

pygame.init()

 # Set screen dimensions

screen_width = 800

```python
screen_height = 600

screen = pygame.display.set_mode((screen_width, screen_height))

pygame.display.set_caption("Resource Management Example")

# Load assets

asset_path = "assets"

background_image = pygame.image.load(os.path.join(asset_path,
"background.jpg")).convert()

player_image = pygame.image.load(os.path.join(asset_path,
"player.png")).convert_alpha()

# Main game loop

running = True

while running:

for event in pygame.event.get():

if event.type == pygame.QUIT:

running = False

# Draw background and player

screen.blit(background_image, (0, 0))

screen.blit(player_image, (screen_width // 2, screen_height // 2))

# Update display

pygame.display.flip()

# Quit Pygame
```

pygame.quit()

In this example, we load background and player images from disk using Pygame's pygame.image.load() function. By converting the images to the appropriate format (convert() for background and convert_alpha() for player), we optimize memory usage and rendering performance on mobile devices.

Conclusion

EFFICIENT RESOURCE management is essential for optimizing performance and ensuring a smooth gaming experience on mobile devices with Pygame. By employing techniques such as texture compression, asset bundling, memory management, streaming, and caching, developers can effectively manage resources and maximize performance, even on devices with limited hardware capabilities.

Distribution on Mobile Platforms

DISTRIBUTING GAMES on mobile platforms presents unique challenges compared to desktop platforms. In this section, we'll explore the process of distributing Pygame games on mobile platforms such as iOS and Android and discuss the various considerations involved.

App Store Submission

SUBMITTING A PYGAME game to the Apple App Store or Google Play Store requires adherence to their respective guidelines and policies. Developers need to create developer accounts, prepare app metadata, screenshots, and promotional materials, and undergo app review processes to ensure compliance with platform requirements.

Platform-Specific Packaging

TO DISTRIBUTE PYGAME games on mobile platforms, developers need to package their games in a format suitable for each platform. For iOS, this typically involves creating an Xcode project, configuring build settings, and generating an IPA (iOS App Store Package) file for submission. On Android, developers package their games as APK (Android Package) files using tools like Android Studio or build systems like Gradle.

Code Signing and Certificates

BEFORE DISTRIBUTING Pygame games on mobile platforms, developers must sign their apps with valid certificates to establish trust and ensure security. On iOS, this involves obtaining a developer certificate and provisioning profiles from the Apple

Developer Portal. On Android, developers sign their APK files with private keys and obtain signing certificates to verify their identity.

Platform-Specific APIs and Requirements

MOBILE PLATFORMS LIKE iOS and Android have their own APIs and requirements that developers must adhere to when distributing Pygame games. These include platform-specific features such as in-app purchases, push notifications, advertising frameworks, and compliance with privacy and data protection regulations like GDPR and COPPA.

Compatibility Testing

ENSURING COMPATIBILITY with different devices, screen sizes, and hardware configurations is crucial when distributing Pygame games on mobile platforms. Developers need to test their games on a variety of devices to identify and address compatibility issues, performance bottlenecks, and platform-specific quirks that may affect the user experience.

Localization and Internationalization

TO REACH A GLOBAL AUDIENCE, developers should consider localizing their Pygame games for different languages and regions. This involves translating in-game text, graphics, and user interfaces into multiple languages and adapting content to suit cultural preferences and sensitivities. Localization and internationalization can enhance accessibility and appeal to diverse audiences worldwide.

Marketing and Promotion

SUCCESSFULLY DISTRIBUTING Pygame games on mobile platforms requires effective marketing and promotion strategies to attract users and drive downloads. Developers can leverage app store optimization (ASO) techniques, social media channels, influencer partnerships, press releases, and promotional campaigns to increase visibility and engagement with their games.

Post-launch Support and Updates

AFTER RELEASING PYGAME games on mobile platforms, developers need to provide ongoing support and updates to address user feedback, bug fixes, and feature requests. Regular updates can help maintain player interest, improve retention rates, and enhance the overall quality and longevity of the game.

Conclusion

DISTRIBUTING PYGAME games on mobile platforms involves careful planning, execution, and adherence to platform-specific guidelines and requirements. By following best practices for app store submission, platform-specific packaging, code signing, compatibility testing, localization, marketing, and post-launch support, developers can maximize their chances of success and reach a wider audience of mobile gamers.

Challenges of Mobile Game Development

DEVELOPING GAMES FOR mobile platforms presents a unique set of challenges compared to desktop or console development. In this section, we'll explore some of the key challenges that developers may encounter when creating mobile games using Pygame.

Device Fragmentation

ONE OF THE BIGGEST challenges in mobile game development is device fragmentation. Unlike desktops or consoles, where hardware and software configurations are relatively standardized, the mobile ecosystem encompasses a wide range of devices with varying screen sizes, resolutions, processing power, and operating system versions. This fragmentation makes it challenging to ensure consistent performance and user experience across different devices.

Touch Input

MOBILE GAMES RELY HEAVILY on touch input for user interaction, which introduces its own set of challenges. Unlike physical controllers or keyboards, touchscreens offer limited tactile feedback and precision, making it harder to design responsive and intuitive controls for mobile games. Developers must carefully consider touch input mechanics and optimize their games for touchscreen devices to provide a smooth and enjoyable gameplay experience.

Performance Optimization

OPTIMIZING PERFORMANCE is critical for mobile game development, especially considering the limited processing power and memory available on mobile devices compared to desktop computers or game consoles. Developers need to employ various optimization techniques such as efficient rendering, texture compression, object pooling, and memory management to ensure smooth frame rates, fast loading times, and minimal battery consumption on mobile platforms.

Battery Life

BATTERY LIFE IS A SIGNIFICANT concern for mobile gamers, particularly for those playing graphically intensive games that consume a lot of CPU and GPU resources. Developers must strike a balance between delivering visually stunning graphics and effects and preserving battery life by optimizing resource usage, minimizing background processes, and implementing power-saving features in their games.

Network Connectivity

MOBILE GAMES OFTEN rely on network connectivity for features such as multiplayer gameplay, social interactions, cloud saves, and in-app purchases. However, maintaining a stable and reliable network connection can be challenging, especially in areas with poor signal coverage or congested networks. Developers need to implement robust networking code, handle network errors gracefully, and provide offline gameplay options to ensure a seamless experience for players.

Monetization Strategies

CHOOSING THE RIGHT monetization strategy is crucial for the success of mobile games, but it can also be challenging given the diverse preferences and behaviors of mobile gamers. Developers need to carefully consider their target audience, market trends, and competition when deciding whether to monetize their games through ads, in-app purchases, subscriptions, or premium pricing models. Balancing monetization with player satisfaction and retention is key to building a sustainable and profitable mobile game business.

App Store Policies and Regulations

NAVIGATING THE POLICIES and regulations of app stores such as the Apple App Store and Google Play Store can be complex and time-consuming. Developers need to familiarize themselves with the rules and guidelines set forth by app store platforms regarding content restrictions, monetization practices, privacy policies, age ratings, and app review processes. Failure to comply with these policies can result in rejection or removal of the game from the app store, impacting its visibility and revenue potential.

Conclusion

DESPITE THE CHALLENGES involved, mobile game development offers immense opportunities for developers to reach a global audience of billions of smartphone users and create innovative and engaging gaming experiences. By addressing the challenges of device fragmentation, touch input, performance optimization, battery life, network connectivity, monetization strategies, and app store regulations, developers can overcome obstacles and create successful mobile games that captivate players and drive revenue.

Virtual Reality and Augmented Reality

Basics of VR and AR in Gaming

VIRTUAL REALITY (VR) and Augmented Reality (AR) are immersive technologies that have gained significant traction in the gaming industry in recent years. While both technologies offer immersive experiences, they differ in their approaches and applications.

Virtual Reality (VR)

VR TECHNOLOGY CREATES a simulated environment that immerses users in a completely virtual world, shutting out the physical surroundings entirely. Users typically wear a VR headset that tracks their head movements and displays stereoscopic 3D visuals to create the illusion of depth and presence. VR gaming allows players to interact with virtual environments and objects using motion controllers or other input devices, providing a highly immersive and engaging experience.

Augmented Reality (AR)

IN CONTRAST TO VR, AR technology overlays digital content onto the real-world environment, blending virtual elements with the physical world in real-time. AR gaming utilizes the camera and sensors on mobile devices or specialized AR glasses to superimpose virtual objects, characters, or information onto the user's view of the real world. AR games often encourage users to interact with virtual objects within their physical surroundings, creating novel and interactive experiences that bridge the gap between the virtual and real worlds.

Applications in Gaming

VR AND AR OFFER UNIQUE opportunities for game developers to create innovative and immersive gaming experiences that transcend traditional gameplay mechanics. VR gaming enables players to fully immerse themselves in virtual worlds, whether exploring fantastical realms, solving puzzles, or engaging in intense action sequences. The sense of presence and immersion provided by VR technology enhances the emotional impact of gaming experiences and enables new forms of storytelling and player interaction.

Similarly, AR gaming integrates digital content seamlessly into the real world, opening up endless possibilities for interactive storytelling, location-based gameplay, and social experiences. AR games encourage players to explore their surroundings, discover hidden treasures, and collaborate with other players in shared augmented spaces. The ability to interact with virtual objects in the context of the real world adds a layer of depth and engagement to gaming experiences, blurring the line between fiction and reality.

Challenges and Considerations

DESPITE THE EXCITING potential of VR and AR in gaming, developers face several challenges and considerations when creating immersive experiences for these platforms. Technical limitations such as hardware requirements, processing power, and tracking accuracy can impact the performance and fidelity of VR and AR games, requiring developers to optimize their code and assets for different devices and platforms.

Moreover, designing compelling VR and AR experiences requires a deep understanding of user interaction, spatial design, and human-computer interfaces. Developers must consider factors such as motion sickness, user comfort, and accessibility when designing VR locomotion systems and AR user interfaces to ensure a seamless and enjoyable experience for players of all ages and abilities.

Additionally, the adoption of VR and AR technology in gaming is still relatively nascent, with challenges such as high costs, limited content availability, and user adoption barriers hindering widespread adoption. Overcoming these challenges will require continued innovation, investment, and collaboration across the gaming industry to democratize access to immersive experiences and unlock the full potential of VR and AR gaming for players worldwide.

Conclusion

IN CONCLUSION, VIRTUAL Reality and Augmented Reality represent exciting frontiers in gaming that promise to revolutionize how we play, experience, and interact with digital content. Whether diving into immersive virtual worlds in VR or overlaying digital elements onto the real world in AR, these technologies offer new opportunities for creativity, storytelling, and social interaction in gaming. By addressing technical challenges, embracing user-centered design principles, and fostering a vibrant ecosystem of content and experiences, developers can unlock the full potential of VR and AR to create compelling and transformative gaming experiences for players of all backgrounds and preferences.

Integrating Pygame with VR and AR Libraries

VIRTUAL REALITY (VR) and Augmented Reality (AR) are rapidly evolving fields with numerous libraries and frameworks available to developers seeking to integrate these technologies into their projects. Pygame, a popular library for game development in Python, can be combined with VR and AR libraries to create immersive gaming experiences that leverage the capabilities of VR headsets and AR devices.

VR Libraries

SEVERAL VR LIBRARIES are compatible with Pygame, allowing developers to create VR applications and games using Python. One such library is **PygameVR**, which provides support for rendering stereoscopic 3D graphics and handling VR input devices such as motion controllers and head-mounted displays. By integrating PygameVR into a Pygame project, developers can leverage the power of VR technology to create immersive gaming experiences that transport players to virtual worlds.

Another popular VR library that can be used alongside Pygame is **OpenVR**, which is developed by Valve Corporation and supports a wide range of VR headsets, including the HTC Vive and Oculus Rift. OpenVR provides a comprehensive API for interacting with VR hardware and rendering 3D graphics, making it suitable for creating VR games and applications with Pygame.

AR Libraries

SIMILARLY, SEVERAL AR libraries are compatible with Pygame, enabling developers to create AR experiences that blend virtual content with the real world. One such library is **PygameAR**, which provides support for overlaying digital content onto live camera feeds and tracking AR markers and objects in real-time. By integrating PygameAR into a Pygame project, developers can create AR games and applications that interact with the user's physical environment.

Another popular AR library that can be used with Pygame is **ARCore**, which is developed by Google and provides support for AR experiences on Android devices. ARCore enables developers to detect flat surfaces, track objects, and place virtual content in the real world, making it suitable for creating AR games and applications for mobile platforms using Pygame.

Integration with Pygame

TO INTEGRATE VR AND AR libraries with Pygame, developers typically need to install the necessary dependencies and configure their projects to support the desired hardware and platforms. This may involve installing SDKs, drivers, and plugins provided by the VR and AR libraries, as well as setting up the appropriate rendering and input systems within Pygame.

Once the libraries are installed and configured, developers can leverage their APIs and functionality to create immersive VR and AR experiences within Pygame. This may involve rendering stereoscopic 3D graphics, handling VR input devices, tracking AR markers, and overlaying virtual content onto live camera feeds, depending on the specific requirements of the project.

Conclusion

IN CONCLUSION, INTEGRATING Pygame with VR and AR libraries opens up exciting possibilities for creating immersive gaming experiences that leverage the capabilities of VR headsets and AR devices. By combining the power and flexibility of Pygame with the features and functionality provided by VR and AR libraries, developers can create compelling VR and AR games and applications that push the boundaries of interactive entertainment. With continued advancements in VR and AR technology and the growing availability of compatible libraries and frameworks, the future looks bright for immersive gaming experiences created with Pygame.

Designing VR and AR Game Experiences

DESIGNING VIRTUAL REALITY (VR) and augmented reality (AR) game experiences requires careful consideration of various factors to ensure an immersive and enjoyable user experience. From user interface design to gameplay mechanics, every aspect of the game must be tailored to the unique capabilities and limitations of VR and AR technology. In this section, we'll explore some key principles and best practices for designing VR and AR game experiences.

Understanding Immersion

IMMERSION IS A KEY aspect of VR and AR game design, as it determines the degree to which players feel present and engaged within the virtual or augmented environment. To create a sense of immersion, developers must leverage the unique capabilities of VR and AR technology, such as stereoscopic 3D graphics, spatial audio, and interactive interfaces. By designing environments and interactions that are convincing and responsive, developers can enhance immersion and draw players deeper into the game world.

Leveraging Spatial Interaction

SPATIAL INTERACTION is another important aspect of VR and AR game design, as it allows players to interact with virtual objects and environments in a natural and intuitive manner. By leveraging motion controllers, hand gestures, and other input devices, developers can enable players to manipulate objects, navigate environments, and perform actions with precision and ease. This enhances the sense of presence and agency within the game world, making the experience more immersive and engaging for players.

Designing for Comfort

COMFORT IS A CRITICAL consideration in VR and AR game design, as discomfort and motion sickness can detract from the overall experience and limit the audience for the game. To minimize discomfort, developers must optimize performance, reduce latency, and implement smooth locomotion and camera movements. Additionally, providing comfort options, such as adjustable movement speeds and teleportation mechanics, can help accommodate players with different comfort preferences and sensitivities.

Ensuring Accessibility

ACCESSIBILITY IS ANOTHER important consideration in VR and AR game design, as it ensures that the game is inclusive and enjoyable for players of all abilities. Developers should design user interfaces and interactions that are easy to understand and navigate, provide alternative control schemes for players with mobility limitations, and offer options for adjusting visual and auditory settings to accommodate players with sensory impairments. By prioritizing accessibility, developers can ensure that their games are accessible to a wider audience and provide a more inclusive gaming experience.

Conclusion

IN CONCLUSION, DESIGNING VR and AR game experiences requires careful consideration of immersion, spatial interaction, comfort, and accessibility. By leveraging the unique capabilities of VR and AR technology and adhering to best practices in game design, developers can create compelling and immersive experiences that captivate players and push the boundaries of interactive entertainment. With continued advancements in VR and AR technology and the growing popularity of immersive gaming experiences, the future looks bright for VR and AR game development.

Challenges in VR/AR Game Development

DEVELOPING VIRTUAL reality (VR) and augmented reality (AR) games presents unique challenges that developers must address to create compelling and immersive experiences. In this section, we'll explore some of the key challenges faced by VR/AR game developers and discuss strategies for overcoming them.

One of the primary challenges in VR/AR game development is hardware fragmentation. Unlike traditional gaming platforms, VR/AR experiences rely on a variety of hardware devices, including headsets, controllers, and tracking systems, each with its own specifications and capabilities. This fragmentation makes it difficult for developers to create games that perform well across all devices and may require them to optimize their games for specific hardware configurations.

Another challenge is locomotion and motion sickness. VR experiences often involve virtual movement within 3D environments, which can cause discomfort and motion sickness for some players, particularly during extended play sessions. To address this challenge, developers must implement comfortable locomotion mechanics, such as teleportation or smooth movement with minimal acceleration, and provide options for adjusting movement settings to suit player preferences.

In addition to locomotion, interaction design is a critical challenge in VR/AR game development. Unlike traditional games, VR/AR experiences allow players to interact with virtual objects and environments in 3D space, requiring developers to design intuitive and responsive interaction systems. This may involve implementing hand tracking, gesture recognition, and physics-based interactions to enable natural and immersive interactions within the game world.

Furthermore, content creation presents a significant challenge for VR/AR game developers. Creating high-quality 3D assets, animations, and environments that are optimized for performance and visual fidelity can be time-consuming and resource-intensive. Additionally, designing levels and gameplay mechanics that take full advantage of the unique affordances of VR/AR technology requires careful planning and iteration.

Another challenge is user experience (UX) design in VR/AR games. Designing user interfaces and interactions that are clear, intuitive, and comfortable to use in immersive 3D environments can be challenging, particularly given the constraints of VR/AR hardware and input devices. Developers must consider factors such as visual hierarchy, spatial layout, and feedback mechanisms to create a seamless and enjoyable user experience.

Finally, distribution and monetization pose challenges for VR/AR game developers. Unlike traditional gaming platforms, VR/AR ecosystems are still relatively nascent and fragmented, making it difficult for developers to reach their target audience and monetize their games effectively. Developers must navigate various distribution channels, such as VR storefronts and app stores, and explore alternative monetization models, such as in-app purchases and subscription services, to maximize the reach and profitability of their games.

In conclusion, VR/AR game development presents a unique set of challenges that require developers to innovate and iterate to create compelling and immersive experiences. By addressing challenges such as hardware fragmentation, locomotion, interaction design, content creation, UX design, and distribution and monetization, developers can overcome obstacles and deliver high-quality VR/AR games that captivate players and push the boundaries of interactive entertainment.

Future of VR and AR in Pygame

THE FUTURE OF VIRTUAL reality (VR) and augmented reality (AR) in Pygame is promising, with continued advancements in technology and growing interest from developers and users alike. As Pygame evolves and new features are added, we can expect to see increased support for VR and AR development, enabling developers to create immersive experiences more easily.

One of the key areas of growth for VR and AR in Pygame is improved support for VR hardware devices, such as headsets and controllers. As VR hardware becomes more accessible and affordable, we can expect Pygame to integrate with a wider range of devices, allowing developers to target a broader audience and create more immersive VR experiences.

In addition to hardware support, we can expect to see advancements in software tools and libraries for VR and AR development in Pygame. This includes libraries for handling spatial tracking, gesture recognition, and 3D audio, as well as tools for creating and importing 3D assets and environments. These advancements will empower developers to create richer and more interactive VR and AR experiences with Pygame.

Furthermore, the future of VR and AR in Pygame will likely involve greater integration with other technologies, such as artificial intelligence (AI) and machine learning (ML). AI and ML algorithms can enhance VR and AR experiences by providing intelligent NPCs, adaptive gameplay mechanics, and personalized content recommendations. By leveraging AI and ML in Pygame, developers can create more dynamic and engaging VR and AR games.

Another area of growth for VR and AR in Pygame is the development of multiplayer and social experiences. As VR and AR technologies become more widespread, we can expect to see an increase in collaborative and social gaming experiences built with Pygame. This includes multiplayer VR games, social VR platforms, and shared AR experiences that enable players to connect and interact with each other in virtual worlds.

Additionally, the future of VR and AR in Pygame will likely involve the exploration of new application domains beyond gaming. VR and AR technologies have the potential to revolutionize fields such as education, healthcare, architecture, and training by providing immersive and interactive simulations. Pygame can play a key role in enabling developers to build applications in these domains and unlock the full potential of VR and AR technology.

Overall, the future of VR and AR in Pygame is bright, with opportunities for innovation and growth in various areas. As Pygame continues to evolve and adapt to the changing landscape of VR and AR technology, we can expect to see a wealth of new experiences and applications that push the boundaries of interactive entertainment and immersive computing.

Chapter 19: Community and Collaboration

Engaging with the Pygame Community

ENGAGING WITH THE PYGAME community is essential for developers looking to learn, collaborate, and grow within the ecosystem. The Pygame community is vibrant and welcoming, with developers of all skill levels contributing to discussions, sharing resources, and collaborating on projects. One of the best ways to engage with the Pygame community is through online forums and discussion groups, such as the official Pygame subreddit, Discord server, and mailing list.

Participating in community events, such as game jams, hackathons, and meetups, is another great way to connect with other Pygame developers and showcase your work. These events provide opportunities to collaborate on projects, receive feedback from peers, and learn from experienced developers. Additionally, participating in community events can help you stay motivated and inspired to continue learning and improving your skills.

Contributing to the Pygame documentation, codebase, and open-source projects is another valuable way to engage with the community and give back to the ecosystem. Whether it's fixing bugs, adding new features, or improving documentation, contributing to Pygame projects helps ensure the continued growth and success of the platform. Plus, contributing to open-source projects is a great way to gain experience, build your portfolio, and establish yourself as a respected member of the community.

Building and sharing your own Pygame projects is an excellent way to engage with the community and showcase your skills. Whether it's a simple game prototype, a library or tool for Pygame development, or a tutorial or blog post sharing your knowledge and insights, sharing your work with the community helps inspire and educate others. Additionally, receiving feedback and constructive criticism from the community can help you improve your projects and grow as a developer.

Finally, supporting and promoting the work of other Pygame developers is essential for building a strong and supportive community. Whether it's sharing interesting projects, providing feedback and encouragement, or collaborating on joint initiatives, supporting your fellow developers helps foster a positive and inclusive community environment. By actively engaging with the Pygame community and contributing to its growth and success, you can play a valuable role in shaping the future of the platform.

Collaborating on Game Projects

COLLABORATING ON GAME projects within the Pygame community can be an enriching experience that allows developers to leverage each other's skills, knowledge, and creativity to create something greater than what they could achieve alone. There are various ways to collaborate on game projects, ranging from informal partnerships between individual developers to organized team efforts on larger-scale projects.

One common approach to collaborating on game projects is through online platforms and communities dedicated to game development. These platforms provide forums, chat rooms, and other communication channels where developers can connect with potential collaborators, share project ideas, and recruit team members. Participating in these communities allows developers to find like-minded individuals with complementary skills and interests, making it easier to form productive collaborations.

Another way to collaborate on game projects is through hackathons and game jams, which are events where developers come together to create games within a limited timeframe, typically ranging from a few days to a week. These events provide a structured environment for collaboration, with teams working together to brainstorm ideas, prototype games, and iterate on designs. Hackathons and game jams encourage creativity, teamwork, and rapid iteration, making them ideal for fostering collaboration within the Pygame community.

Forming development teams with specific roles and responsibilities is another effective way to collaborate on game projects. By dividing tasks such as programming, art, music, and level design among team members, developers can leverage each other's strengths and expertise to create well-rounded and polished games. Tools such as version control systems and project management software can help teams coordinate their efforts, track progress, and communicate effectively throughout the development process.

In addition to formal collaborations, developers can also benefit from informal mentorship and guidance from more experienced members of the Pygame community. Seeking out experienced developers for advice, feedback, and code reviews can help less experienced developers improve their skills, avoid common pitfalls, and learn best practices for game development. Mentorship can take many forms, from one-on-one mentoring relationships to participation in online forums and communities where experienced developers share their knowledge and insights with others.

Ultimately, collaborating on game projects within the Pygame community is not only a great way to create compelling games but also an opportunity to learn, grow, and connect with other developers who share a passion for game development. Whether you're working on a small hobby project with a friend or contributing to a large-scale open-source game, collaborating with others can enrich your development experience and help you achieve your goals as a game developer.

Contributing to Pygame Development

CONTRIBUTING TO THE development of Pygame itself is a rewarding way to give back to the community and help improve the framework for everyone. Pygame is an open-source project, which means that anyone can contribute code, documentation, bug fixes, or other improvements. Contributing to Pygame development can take many forms, from submitting bug reports and feature requests to writing code patches and documentation.

One of the most accessible ways to contribute to Pygame is by reporting bugs and issues that you encounter while using the framework. By providing detailed information about the problem, including steps to reproduce it and any relevant error messages or stack traces, you can help the Pygame development team identify and fix bugs more quickly. Bug reports can be submitted through the Pygame issue tracker on GitHub, where they will be reviewed by the development team and prioritized for resolution.

Another way to contribute to Pygame is by submitting patches or pull requests that address existing issues or add new features to the framework. Before submitting a patch, it's important to familiarize yourself with the Pygame development process and coding conventions, as well as the existing codebase and architecture. This will help ensure that your contributions are in line with the project's goals and standards and increase the likelihood that they will be accepted by the development team.

In addition to writing code patches, you can also contribute to Pygame by improving documentation, writing tutorials, or creating examples and demos that showcase how to use the framework. Clear and comprehensive documentation is essential for helping new users get started with Pygame and for providing guidance on best practices and advanced techniques. By contributing to the documentation, you can help make Pygame more accessible and user-friendly for developers of all skill levels.

If you're interested in contributing to Pygame development but don't know where to start, consider joining the Pygame community and participating in discussions on the Pygame mailing list, forums, or IRC channel. Engaging with other developers and learning from their experiences can help you become more familiar with the project and identify areas where you can contribute effectively. You can also reach out to the Pygame development team or experienced community members for guidance and mentorship as you begin your journey as a Pygame contributor.

Overall, contributing to Pygame development is a valuable way to support the project and help shape its future direction. Whether you're fixing bugs, adding new features, or improving documentation, your contributions can have a positive impact on the Pygame community and help ensure that the framework continues to thrive and evolve for years to come.

Learning from Open Source Game Projects

STUDYING OPEN-SOURCE game projects is an excellent way to learn from real-world examples and gain insights into game development best practices, techniques, and workflows. Open-source games provide valuable resources that you can explore, analyze, and even contribute to, helping you improve your own game development skills and understanding.

One of the primary benefits of studying open-source game projects is the opportunity to examine their source code and architecture. By exploring how different components of a game are implemented, such as graphics rendering, input handling, or game logic, you can gain a deeper understanding of how games work and how to structure your own projects more effectively. You can also learn about common patterns and techniques used in game development, such as entity-component systems, state machines, or event-driven architectures.

In addition to source code, many open-source game projects also provide documentation, tutorials, and other educational resources that can help you learn new skills and techniques. By following along with tutorials or studying documentation, you can learn how to use specific tools, libraries, or frameworks in your own projects and gain practical experience working with them. You can also find examples of how to implement specific features or mechanics, such as multiplayer networking, procedural generation, or artificial intelligence, which you can adapt and integrate into your own games.

Another benefit of studying open-source game projects is the opportunity to collaborate with other developers and contribute to the project's development. By participating in discussions, submitting bug reports or feature requests, and even submitting code patches or pull requests, you can engage with the project's community and make meaningful contributions to its growth and improvement. This collaborative aspect of open-source development can be a valuable learning experience and can help you develop your communication, teamwork, and problem-solving skills.

Furthermore, studying open-source game projects can provide inspiration and ideas for your own game projects. By exploring a variety of different games, genres, and styles, you can discover new gameplay mechanics, art styles, or narrative techniques that you can incorporate into your own games. You can also learn from the successes and failures of other projects, gaining insights into what works well and what doesn't in game design and development.

Overall, studying open-source game projects is a valuable learning opportunity for aspiring game developers. By exploring source code, documentation, and other resources, collaborating with other developers, and seeking inspiration from existing projects, you can improve your skills, expand your knowledge, and become a more confident and capable game developer.

Hosting Game Jams and Competitions

HOSTING GAME JAMS AND competitions is a fantastic way to foster creativity, collaboration, and innovation within the game development community. Game jams are events where participants have a limited amount of time, typically ranging from a few days to a week, to create a game from scratch based on a specific theme or set of constraints. Competitions, on the other hand, may have longer development periods and often focus on specific genres, mechanics, or technical challenges.

One of the key benefits of hosting game jams and competitions is the opportunity to bring together developers of all skill levels and backgrounds to work on creative projects and share their work with others. Game jams often attract a diverse range of participants, including hobbyists, students, indie developers, and professionals, all of whom can contribute unique perspectives, ideas, and expertise to the event. This diversity of talent can lead to the creation of innovative and original games that push the boundaries of game design and technology.

Another benefit of hosting game jams and competitions is the sense of community and camaraderie that they foster among participants. Game development can often be a solitary pursuit, but events like game jams provide an opportunity for developers to collaborate, share ideas, and support one another in a collaborative and inclusive environment. Participants can form teams, join online communities, and engage in discussions and feedback sessions to help each other overcome challenges and improve their skills.

Hosting game jams and competitions can also be a valuable learning experience for participants, providing them with an opportunity to practice their game development skills, experiment with new tools and techniques, and receive feedback from their peers and mentors. Participants can learn valuable lessons about time management, project planning, and team collaboration, as well as gain insights into the iterative process of game development and the importance of playtesting and iteration.

Furthermore, game jams and competitions can be a great way to showcase and promote indie games and emerging talent within the game development community. By providing a platform for developers to share their creations with a wider audience, these events can help to elevate the visibility of indie games and increase awareness of new and innovative projects. Hosting competitions with prizes or awards can also incentivize participation and motivate developers to push themselves creatively and technically.

In addition to benefiting individual developers, hosting game jams and competitions can also have broader impacts on the game development community as a whole. By encouraging collaboration, experimentation, and creative expression, these events contribute to the overall growth and evolution of the medium, inspiring new ideas, trends, and approaches to game design and development. They also help to build connections and foster relationships within the industry, leading to future collaborations, partnerships, and opportunities for professional development and growth.

Overall, hosting game jams and competitions is a rewarding and impactful way to support and celebrate the game development community. By providing a platform for creativity, collaboration, and innovation, these events help to cultivate talent, promote diversity, and push the boundaries of what is possible in game design and development. Whether you're a seasoned developer or just starting out, participating in or hosting a game jam or competition can be a fun and fulfilling experience that brings people together and inspires creativity.

Chapter 20: Beyond Pygame: Next Steps in Game Development

Enhancing Pygame with Other Game Development Frameworks and Engines

AS YOU PROGRESS IN your game development journey, you may find yourself wanting to explore other game development frameworks and engines beyond Pygame. While Pygame is a powerful and versatile tool for creating 2D games, there are many other options available that offer different features, capabilities, and workflows to suit your needs and preferences.

Unity

UNITY IS ONE OF THE most popular game development engines in the world, known for its versatility, ease of use, and robust feature set. While Unity is primarily used for creating 3D games, it also supports 2D game development through its dedicated 2D tools and workflows. Unity provides a wide range of features, including built-in physics, animation, audio, and visual effects tools, as well as support for multiple platforms, including PC, console, mobile, and web. Unity also has a large and active community of developers and resources, making it easy to find tutorials, assets, and support online.

Unreal Engine

UNREAL ENGINE IS ANOTHER powerful and widely used game development engine, particularly well-suited for creating high-fidelity 3D games and immersive experiences. Unreal Engine offers advanced graphics rendering capabilities, including real-time ray tracing, as well as built-in tools for animation, audio, and visual effects. Unreal Engine also supports a wide range of platforms, including PC, console, mobile, and virtual reality (VR). While Unreal Engine has a steeper learning curve compared to other engines, it provides unparalleled flexibility and control over every aspect of your game.

Godot Engine

GODOT ENGINE IS A FREE and open-source game development engine that is gaining popularity for its simplicity, flexibility, and community-driven development model. Godot Engine is particularly well-suited for creating 2D and 3D games, with a focus on ease of use and performance. It features a visual scripting language called GDScript, as well as support for popular programming languages like C# and Python. Godot Engine also provides built-in tools for animation, physics, audio, and visual effects, as well as support for multiple platforms, including PC, mobile, and web.

Construct

CONSTRUCT IS A BROWSER-based game development tool that is designed for creating 2D games without the need for programming. Construct uses a visual scripting interface that allows you to create games by dragging and dropping elements onto a canvas and connecting them together. Construct provides a wide range of built-in features and behaviors, including physics, animation, audio, and visual effects, as well as support for exporting games to multiple platforms, including PC, mobile, and web. Construct is a great option for beginners and hobbyists who want to create games quickly and easily without writing code.

Phaser

PHASER IS A FAST, FREE, and open-source game development framework for creating HTML5 games. Phaser is particularly well-suited for creating 2D games that run in web browsers, with support for features like sprites, animations, physics, audio, and input handling. Phaser provides a flexible and modular architecture that allows you to create games using JavaScript and other web technologies, as well as a rich ecosystem of plugins and extensions. Phaser is a great choice for developers who want to create web-based games that can be played on a wide range of devices and platforms.

Other Frameworks and Engines

IN ADDITION TO THE options mentioned above, there are many other game development frameworks and engines available that offer different features, capabilities, and workflows. Some other popular options include Cocos2d, GameMaker Studio, Love2D, and libGDX. Ultimately, the best framework or engine for your game will depend on your specific needs, goals, and preferences, so it's worth exploring different options and experimenting with them to find the right fit for your project.

Transitioning from Pygame to More Advanced Engines

TRANSITIONING FROM Pygame to more advanced game engines can be a daunting but rewarding journey for game developers looking to take their skills to the next level. While Pygame is a great tool for learning the basics of game development and creating simple 2D games, advanced engines offer a wider range of features, tools, and capabilities for creating more complex and polished games.

One of the key differences between Pygame and more advanced engines is the level of abstraction and complexity they offer. Pygame provides a relatively low-level interface to game development, requiring developers to handle many aspects of game development, such as rendering, physics, and audio, manually. In contrast, advanced engines like Unity and Unreal Engine abstract away many of these low-level details, providing higher-level tools and workflows that streamline the game development process.

Another important consideration when transitioning to more advanced engines is the learning curve involved. While Pygame is relatively easy to learn and use, advanced engines like Unity and Unreal Engine have steeper learning curves due to their complexity and feature-richness. Developers may need to invest time and effort into learning the ins and outs of these engines, including their proprietary scripting languages, editor workflows, and best practices for game development.

However, the payoff for mastering more advanced engines can be significant. These engines offer a wide range of features and capabilities that can help developers create more visually stunning, immersive, and engaging games. From advanced graphics rendering and physics simulations to built-in tools for animation, audio, and visual effects, advanced engines provide everything developers need to bring their game ideas to life.

One of the main advantages of transitioning to more advanced engines is the ability to target a wider range of platforms and devices. While Pygame is primarily used for creating desktop games, advanced engines like Unity and Unreal Engine support multiple platforms, including PC, console, mobile, and web. This allows developers to reach a larger audience and potentially increase the success and visibility of their games.

Another advantage of using more advanced engines is the wealth of resources and support available. These engines have large and active communities of developers who share knowledge, tutorials, assets, and plugins to help each other succeed. From official documentation and tutorials to community forums and online courses, developers have access to a wealth of resources to help them learn, troubleshoot, and optimize their games.

Overall, transitioning from Pygame to more advanced engines can be a challenging but rewarding experience for game developers. By mastering these engines, developers can unlock new possibilities for their games and take their skills to the next level. Whether you're interested in creating 3D games, targeting multiple platforms, or pushing the boundaries of what's possible in game development, advanced engines offer the tools and capabilities you need to succeed.

Further Learning Resources

CONTINUING TO LEARN and improve your game development skills is essential for staying competitive and creating high-quality games. Fortunately, there are many resources available to help you further your knowledge and expertise in game development. Whether you're looking to learn new programming languages, explore advanced game design concepts, or master specific game development tools and technologies, there's something out there for everyone.

One of the best ways to continue learning is through online courses and tutorials. Websites like Udemy, Coursera, and Pluralsight offer a wide range of courses on game development topics, including programming, game design, graphics, and audio. These courses are taught by industry professionals and cover both beginner and advanced topics, making them suitable for developers of all skill levels.

Books are another valuable resource for learning game development. There are countless books available on game programming, game design, game art, and other aspects of game development. Whether you prefer digital or physical books, you're sure to find plenty of resources to help you deepen your understanding of game development concepts and techniques.

Online communities and forums are also great places to learn from others and get support and feedback on your projects. Websites like Stack Overflow, Reddit, and gamedev.net have active communities of game developers who are eager to share their knowledge and help others succeed. Participating in these communities can be a great way to connect with other developers, learn from their experiences, and get answers to your questions.

Additionally, attending game development conferences and events can provide valuable opportunities to learn from industry experts, network with other developers, and stay up-to-date on the latest trends and technologies in game development. Conferences like the Game Developers Conference (GDC), IndieCade, and PAX offer a wide range of talks, panels, and workshops on game development topics.

Finally, don't forget to practice, experiment, and apply what you've learned in your own projects. The best way to solidify your understanding of game development concepts and techniques is to use them in real-world projects. Start small, work on projects that interest you, and don't be afraid to make mistakes. With time and persistence, you'll continue to grow and improve as a game developer.

Building a Portfolio and Getting Involved in the Industry

BUILDING A PORTFOLIO is crucial for aspiring game developers looking to break into the industry. Your portfolio showcases your skills, creativity, and passion for game development, and it's often the first thing potential employers or collaborators will look at when considering you for a job or project. Here are some tips for creating a strong game development portfolio:

1. **Showcase Your Best Work:** Choose a selection of your best projects to include in your portfolio. These could be games you've created, game prototypes, game jams, or any other relevant work. Make sure to highlight your role in each project and provide context about the project's goals, challenges, and outcomes.

2. **Diversify Your Portfolio:** Include a variety of projects in your portfolio to demonstrate your versatility as a game developer. This could include games of different genres, styles, and platforms, as well as projects that showcase your skills in programming, game design, art, sound, and other areas of game development.

3. **Provide Context and Documentation:** For each project in your portfolio, provide clear and concise descriptions that explain what the project is about, what technologies and tools were used, and any interesting challenges or accomplishments you encountered during development. Include screenshots, videos, and other visual assets to help showcase your work.

4. **Keep It Updated:** Regularly update your portfolio with new projects and experiences as you continue to grow and develop as a game developer. Remove outdated or

irrelevant projects to keep your portfolio focused and up-to-date.

5. **Seek Feedback:** Before sharing your portfolio with others, ask for feedback from friends, mentors, or members of the game development community. Constructive feedback can help you identify areas for improvement and make your portfolio more effective.

6. **Promote Your Portfolio:** Once you've created your portfolio, share it with potential employers, collaborators, and anyone else who may be interested in your work. You can share your portfolio through your personal website, social media channels, online forums, and networking events.

Getting involved in the game development industry can be challenging, but there are many ways to increase your chances of success. Here are some tips for getting involved in the industry:

1. **Networking:** Networking is key to finding opportunities and building relationships within the game development community. Attend industry events, conferences, and meetups, join online forums and communities, and connect with other developers on social media platforms like Twitter, LinkedIn, and Discord.

2. **Volunteer and Internship Opportunities:** Look for volunteer and internship opportunities at game studios, indie game projects, and game development events. Volunteering or interning can provide valuable experience, help you build your network, and open doors to future job opportunities.

3. **Freelancing:** Consider offering your services as a freelance game developer, artist, designer, or musician. Freelancing can be a great way to gain experience, build your portfolio,

and earn income while working on a variety of projects.

4. **Contributing to Open Source Projects:** Contributing to open source game projects is a great way to learn new skills, collaborate with other developers, and gain visibility within the game development community. Look for open source projects on platforms like GitHub and GitLab and contribute code, documentation, or other resources.

5. **Continuous Learning:** Stay up-to-date on the latest trends, technologies, and best practices in game development by regularly reading blogs, articles, and books, watching tutorials and lectures, and participating in online courses and workshops. Continuous learning is essential for staying competitive and advancing your career in game development.

By following these tips and actively seeking out opportunities to learn, grow, and connect with others in the game development community, you can increase your chances of success and achieve your goals in the industry.

Future Trends in Game Development

GAME DEVELOPMENT IS an ever-evolving field, driven by technological advancements, changing consumer preferences, and emerging trends. Staying informed about these trends can help developers anticipate the direction of the industry and adapt their skills and strategies accordingly. Here are some future trends in game development to keep an eye on:

1. **Virtual Reality (VR) and Augmented Reality (AR):** VR and AR technologies continue to gain traction in the gaming industry, offering immersive experiences that blur the line between the virtual and physical worlds. As VR and AR hardware becomes more affordable and accessible, we can expect to see an increase in VR and AR games and applications across various platforms.
2. **Cloud Gaming:** Cloud gaming services, which allow players to stream games over the internet instead of downloading and installing them locally, are becoming increasingly popular. As internet infrastructure improves and streaming technology advances, cloud gaming could revolutionize how games are distributed, played, and monetized.
3. **Artificial Intelligence (AI):** AI technology is playing an increasingly important role in game development, powering non-player characters (NPCs), creating more realistic behaviors and interactions, and enhancing game experiences through procedural generation and adaptive difficulty. As AI algorithms become more sophisticated and accessible, we can expect to see AI-driven gameplay mechanics and narratives in future games.
4. **Cross-Platform Play and Progression:** With the growing

popularity of multiplayer and online games, there is a growing demand for cross-platform play and progression, allowing players to seamlessly switch between different devices and platforms while retaining their progress and achievements. Cross-platform support is becoming increasingly common and is expected to become standard in future games.

5. **User-Generated Content:** User-generated content (UGC) has become a powerful force in game development, allowing players to create and share their own levels, mods, skins, and other content within games. As tools for creating UGC become more accessible and integrated into game development platforms, we can expect to see more games embrace UGC as a way to extend the lifespan and replayability of their games.

6. **Blockchain and NFTs:** Blockchain technology and non-fungible tokens (NFTs) have the potential to disrupt the gaming industry by enabling true ownership of in-game assets, creating decentralized economies, and empowering players to monetize their gaming experiences. While still in its early stages, blockchain gaming could revolutionize how games are created, distributed, and monetized in the future.

7. **Ethical and Inclusive Game Design:** With increased awareness of social issues and ethical concerns in the gaming industry, there is a growing emphasis on ethical and inclusive game design practices. Future games are likely to prioritize diversity, representation, accessibility, and responsible monetization strategies to create more inclusive and socially responsible gaming experiences.

8. **Environmental Sustainability:** As concerns about climate change and environmental sustainability continue to grow,

there is a growing push for greener and more sustainable practices in game development. Future games are likely to prioritize energy efficiency, minimize carbon footprints, and explore eco-friendly themes and narratives.

By staying informed about these future trends and embracing new technologies and practices, game developers can position themselves for success in an ever-changing and dynamic industry.

www.ingramcontent.com/pod-product-compliance
Lightning Source LLC
Chambersburg PA
CBHW021144160726
47994CB00001B/74